GOD, PRAYER, REDEMPTION, AND HOPE
PASTORAL AND THEOLOGICAL REFLECTIONS

GOD, PRAYER, REDEMPTION, AND HOPE

PASTORAL AND THEOLOGICAL REFLECTIONS

R. Hollis Gause

CHEROHALA PRESS
CLEVELAND, TENNESSEE

God, Prayer, Redemption, and Hope
Pastoral and Theological Reflections

Published by Cherohala Press
900 Walker ST NE
Cleveland, TN 37311
USA
email. cptpress@pentecostaltheology.org

Library of Congress Control Number: 2016949732

ISBN-10 1935931571
ISBN-13 9781935931577

Copyright © 2016 Cherohala Press

Cover art 'The Crucifixion of Jesus', by Gustave Doré

All rights reserved. No part of this book may be reproduced or transmitted in any form or by any means, electronic or mechanical, including photocopying, recording, or by any information storage or retrieval system, without permission in writing from the publisher. For information, contact us at CPT Press, 900 Walker ST NE, Cleveland, TN 37311, or online at www.cptpress.com.

Most CPT Press books are available at special quantity discounts when purchased in bulk by bookstores, organizations, and special-interest groups. For more information, please e-mail cptpress@pentecostaltheology.org.

TABLE OF CONTENTS

1. To Save a Life 1
2. Love Casts Out Fear 3
3. Prepare the Way of the Lord 5
4. Reformation Sunday 7
5. The Cost of Discipleship 9
6. Restoration 11
7. Praise Ye the Lord 13
8. Breaking a Bruised Reed 15
9. God is Love 17
10. The Drama of Redemption 19
11. From the Manger to the Cross 21
12. The New Year 23
13. Human Merit 25
14. Pray for Our President 27
15. How to Cultivate Faith 29
16. Personal Significance 31
17. Be Anxious for Nothing 33
18. What is Prayer? 35
19. Holiness and Christ's Return 37
20. What Is the Measure of Greatness? 39
21. Jesus Passed by 41
22. Father, Forgive Them 43
23. Christ Is Risen 45
24. What Does the Resurrection Mean for Us? 47
25. Right Is not Might 49
26. Mother's Day 51
27. The Courage of the Obedience of Faith 53
28. God in the Hands of an Angry Sinner 55

29. Prayer as Moral Duty and Privilege 57
30. To See the Best and Accept the Second Best 59
31. You Are the Epistle of Christ 61
32. You Can't Box with God 63
33. Proclaim Liberty 65
34. We Have Found the Messiah 67
35. God Is Faithful 69
36. What Belongs to God; What Belongs to Caesar? ... 71
37. God Will Supply Our Needs 73
38. Nothing in My Hand I Bring 75
39. So, You Are a Free Moral Agent? 77
40. What Kind of Preacher Are You? 79
41. What Is Revival? 81
42. Enemy in the Home 83
43. This Is the Lord's Table 85
44. No Weapon that Is Formed against You 87
45. Where There Is no Vision the People Perish 89
46. Help, I Need Prayer 91
47. The Deadness of Self Preservation 93
48. Prayer 95
49. Are Prayers just Pious Nonsense? 99
50. Let Christ Be Lifted Up 101
51. Safety and Security 103
52. Atonement 105
53. The Gospel in Miniature 107
54. Christ's Return 109
55. The Journey of the Magi 111
56. Encounter with Greatness 113
57. Christ in You the Hope of Glory 115
58. Journey to the Kingdom... 117
59. A Burning Coal from the Altar (Isaiah 6) 121
60. A Parable of Christmas... 125

Index of Biblical References.. 127

1

TO SAVE A LIFE

The story has been told of two foot-travelers in the Himalayan Mountains. They were overtaken by the cold of the night before they could reach their destination and safety.

As they traveled, they heard the cry of an injured traveler. One of the travelers reasoned that if they stopped and rescued the injured man, they themselves would be caught in the cold of the night. The rescue attempt might cost them injury or even death. So he went on determined to save his own life.

The other traveler could not pass by the injured man and leave him to almost certain death from exposure and injury. He delayed his journey, lifted the injured stranger out of the snow, placed him on his own shoulders, and proceeded to his destination. His arrival was delayed and was even more tortuous because of his additional burden.

The burden of carrying the injured man had increased his circulation and body warmth. He made it to safety; he had saved the life of another and his own life by his act of compassion.

His companion who had gone ahead with no additional burden was later found frozen to death within sight of home.

Jesus said, 'For whoever wishes to save his life shall destroy it, but whoever loses his life for my sake shall save it' (Matthew 16.25).

2

LOVE CASTS OUT FEAR

Stop trying to calm fear with information! It is love that casts out fear. Every parent knows that a warm hug calms a child more than a verbal explanation.

'Love is patient; it is kind; love is not zealous for self; it does not brag; it is not self-inflated; it does not act unbecomingly; it does not demand its own things' (1 Corinthians 13.4, 5). Love such as this flows from the heart of God and is poured out in our hearts by the Holy Spirit who has been given to us (Romans 5.5).

To live by love is a more excellent way of life than to exercise the gifts of the Holy Spirit. There might be an apparent outward display of these gifts only to have them clang as a cymbal without the quality of love. There might be the outward exercise of what passes as Christian charity only to be rendered nothing in the absence of love.

Love abides when the need for prophecy, tongues, and knowledge yield their place to the coming of that which is perfect – the fulfilled kingdom of God in Christ. Love is the very fabric of that estate and endures in the eternity of God's kingdom. It is the kingdom of love – purchased by love, permeated by love, and enduring by love.

Of all spiritual graces love is the greatest (1 Corinthians 13.13). It is the band around all the rest of the fruit of the Spirit, giving the fruit its fulfillment and perfection. 'Keep on seeking love' (1 Corinthians 14.1). 'Perfect love casts out fear' (1 John 4.18).

3

PREPARE THE WAY OF THE LORD

John the Baptist was the herald of the King. In ancient times the herald of the king would go before the king and announce to the people that their king would pass through their area. He would tell them to prepare for the king's coming. 'On such an occasion to make a "king's highway" valleys had to be filled, hills leveled, bypaths straightened.' [*Cambridge Greek Testament*]

Isaiah said of the coming of the King of glory, 'Every valley shall be exalted, and every mountain and hill shall be made low; and the crooked shall be made straight, and the rough places plain' (Isaiah 40.4).

'Prepare ye the way of the Lord' was John's message. The way of the Lord is the way of holiness. The call to repentance is a call to restore to its proper standard this way of the Lord. John applied his message to religious leaders, to the common people, to publicans, to soldiers, and to all others who came under his ministry. Obstacles lay in the way of the King. The way to clear a path for His coming is repentance. It is the same today.

Repentance is always a personal encounter with God. It originates when God convicts the individual of sin. It is the individual's response to this act of divine grace to correct his/her own way in the fear of God.

To those who do not know Christ as Savior, this is a crisis call. To those who already know Christ, the call to repentance is a perpetual call and demand. It is a way of living in Christ. It is an essential for renewal, and life that is not in continual renewal will die.

6

4

REFORMATION SUNDAY

Today is Reformation Sunday. What does that mean? It has historical and spiritual significance. Historically, the Protestant Reformation began in the sixteenth century. Martin Luther, a Roman Catholic priest, led the attack first within the Roman Catholic Church and later separated from the Roman Catholic Church. One of the most dramatic events in this movement was the posting of Luther's ninety-five theses for debate at Wittenberg. The debate which followed led to the break between the Roman Catholic Church and the 'protesters'. Out of this beginning we have the Protestant church movement.

What is a Protestant? A 'protester'? He/she is that, but more than that. A Protestant is a witness, specifically a witness to specific biblical truths that had been neglected in the theology and worship of the Roman Catholic Church.

The heart of the Protestant witness/protest consists of three fundamental claims.
1. The Bible is the word of God and has authority over the church, its membership, its offices, and its teachings.
2. Every believer in Jesus Christ is a priest (the priesthood of all believers). Every believer has immediate (rather than mediated) access to the throne of grace to receive mercy and help in time of need.

3. Believers are justified by faith and not by works. Justification includes the forgiveness of all past sins and acceptance as righteous in Jesus Christ.

The Pentecostal movement arose within the Protestant movement and brought other emphases in doctrine and spiritual freedom. One of the most important of these is the prophethood of all believers. The promise of Joel is that the Spirit of God would be poured out on all flesh. men, women, bond, free, young, and old. All of these shall prophesy. As all believers are priests, they are also prophets – witnesses of God's grace.

We celebrate the historical heritage, but more than that we celebrate the spiritual heritage with the renewed emphasis on Pentecostal witness.

5

THE COST OF DISCIPLESHIP

Our Lord took great pain to show us the difficult side of discipleship. Christ wanted those who followed Him to understand the cost of discipleship. 'Or what king, going to make war against another king, sitteth not down first, and consulteth whether he be able with ten thousand to meet him that cometh against him with twenty thousand?' (Luke 14.31).

Jesus also wants us to know how to interpret hardship when it comes. The Scriptures assure us that hardship comes with discipleship. 'All that will live godly in Christ Jesus will suffer persecution' (2 Timothy 3.12). There is a blessedness in this. 'If ye be reproached for the name of Christ, happy are ye' (1 Peter 4.14).

The consciousness of this blessedness is reflected throughout the New Testament. Jesus shows this in the Sermon on the Mount in the Beatitudes (Matthew 5.3-12). The word translated 'happy' in 1 Peter 4.14 is the same word that is translated 'blessed' in the Beatitudes. Paul considered persecution for Christ's sake to be a gift of God's grace. 'For unto you it is given in the behalf of Christ not only to believe on him, but also to suffer for his sake' (Philippians 1.29).

Some aspects of the blessedness are described in 1 Peter 4.13, 14. We are partakers of Christ's sufferings (v. 13). We shall be glad when Christ appears in His glory (v. 13b), and the 'Spirit of glory and of God resteth upon us' (v. 14). Philippians 3.10, 11 tell us that if we would know Christ in the power of His resurrection, we must also know Him in the fellowship of His sufferings. If we suffer with Him we shall be glorified with Him (Romans 8.17).

6

RESTORATION

The gospel of Christ is a message of restoration from the God who restores. God set the pattern in the restoration of the fallen race. He restores the unregenerate and the backsliding.

One of the characteristics of the spiritual person is that she/he applies the principles of restoration in personal relationships. This does not mean that we ignore sin or excuse it. There is a vast difference between forgiving sin and excusing it. It does mean that our attitude toward sin and the sinner can reflect God's attitude toward sin and the sinner.

If the church behaves in a biblical manner toward the person who falls away, this offender can be restored so fully that the remembrance of his/her fall can be virtually erased. The glory of this act is that it can be done without compromise; in fact, forgiveness is a fundamental act of holiness.

There are sound biblical reasons for this behavior. First, the receivers of mercy must give mercy. Second, those who are subject to failure must not stand in haughty and unrelenting judgment of those who are victims of temptation. Instead they should remain humble lest they 'also be tempted' (Galatians 6.1). Third, this is the way God reigns in His kingdom (Matthew 6.12; Luke 11.4). God rules in grace by forgiving.

7

PRAISE YE THE LORD

The Lord Jesus was worshiped and praised by angels on the night of His birth.

He was praised by the throngs shouting 'Hosanna' as He entered Jerusalem.

He was praised by the waiting church on the day of Pentecost.

He will return amidst the praises of ten thousands of His saints.

The summation of this is that when God is being praised, marvelous

Things are happening, and God is doing them.
> He is saving men and women.
> He is reigning in His kingdom.
> He is pouring out His Spirit.
> Christ is returning in glory.

The vision in Revelation sees and hears this praise and has recorded it for us. 'Every created thing which is in heaven, or on earth, and under the earth, and on the sea, and all things that are in them, heard I saying, unto Him that sitteth on the throne, and unto the Lamb, be the blessing and the honour and the glory, and the dominion forever and ever' (Revelation 5.13).

8

BREAKING A BRUISED REED

'A bruised reed shall he not break, and a smoking flax shall he not quench …' (Isaiah 42.3). Two men in the New Testament stand out as illustrations of this truth about Christ – Joseph of Arimathaea and Nicodemus.

We do not know when Joseph became acquainted with Jesus, but we do know when he made his discipleship known publicly. It was in the darkest hour for Christians – the occasion of the death of our Lord. The outspoken and stalwart Simon Peter had just denied the Lord. Others of the disciples – even the Apostles – were discouraged. Some distanced themselves from Jesus. It was under these circumstances of crisis and personal danger that Joseph made his discipleship known.

Our first acquaintance with Nicodemus is that night during a Passover season when he visited Jesus (John 3). Then Christ explained to him the new birth – its nature and necessity. The seed of the new birth was planted in that night. From that time until the trial and death of Jesus Nicodemus was intimidated from making his faith public. The crisis of our Lord's trial and crucifixion brought it out.

It is not for us to answer all the questions that arise from such conversions and timidity of testimony. Neither is it for us to deny the truth of such conversions. Much more, it is not men and women to quench such converts by ridicule and scorn.

The bruised reed that Christ will not break and smoldering flax that He will not douse are the objects of His care. Let them also become the subjects of the church's prayers and care.

9

GOD IS LOVE

'God is love' (1 John 4.16). This description of God covers all that we need to say about the holiness of God. In the same way love is the one spiritual grace that exceeds all others in the human heart. It is our kinship with God, our dwelling in Him and His dwelling in us. Love is the ground upon which God acts and speaks, and it characterizes all that He does and says. Therefore, it is to become for us the ground of our existence and the motive for all that we say and do.

Love is the highest dignity of the human soul. God could have exalted humankind no higher than to give them the capacity to love, and to let them realize the sublime experience of loving. Love is not only the fulfillment of the law of God it is the fulfillment of the nature of humankind.

In the light of these considerations we must conclude that sin is committed when we fail to love. Hatred is the most extreme violation of love and distortion of human nature. There are other distortions of human nature that come short of the extreme of hatred. The failure to love is sinful. This is also degrading to the human soul and is foreign to the nature of God.

The Christmas season is a celebration of love. We celebrate God's great act of giving His only begotten Son. It is appropriate that we give to those who will return our love. It is also appropriate that we give to those who may not return our love – even to those who reject and spurn our love. This is the way God loved us; let us be followers of God as dear children.

There are many opportunities to give in this manner. We can give to the poor through charities, the church, and directly. We can give our time and energy to ease the load of someone in need, such as the elderly, the sick, the poor, the derelict, the imprisoned, and many others. We can scrub a floor, sweep a sidewalk, cook a meal, visit the sick or the imprisoned. There are many ways to give ourselves; let us follow our Lord in finding them.

10

THE DRAMA OF REDEMPTION

The gospel of Christ is the most dramatic theme in world history. Christmas celebrates a climaxing point in this drama. The central message is, 'For God so loved the world that he gave his only begotten Son that whosoever believeth in him should not perish, but have everlasting life' (John 3.16).

The human characters in this drama are demonstrations of the grace of God, and they have their places in it by believing God. Mary was not chosen to give birth to the Messiah because she was the best or purest woman in all of Israel. She was chosen for this role because she 'found grace with God' (Luke 1.30). In God's act of grace toward her the Holy Spirit overshadowed her as the glory of God over the tabernacle in the wilderness (Luke 1.35). For Mary this miracle of grace called on her to believe God, and she was blessed of God for having believed (Luke 1.45). The story of the virgin birth is the message of grace to Mary and to all humankind.

Joseph was a devout man who loved the law of God and Mary his espoused wife. Mary's being found with child tore him between these two loves. As a devout man he felt obligated to divorce her (Matthew 1.18, 19). His love for Mary moved him to protect her if he could. Here is a rare combination of grace. 'Mercy and truth are met together; righteousness and peace have kissed each other' (Psalm 85.10).

Joseph obeyed God at great personal sacrifice. Few people would believe the story of a virgin birth. Most would conclude that Joseph was the father, especially if he kept the marriage. His own integrity in the eyes of the community was at stake. People would doubt that he was a man of pure morals. Would he respond to God or to the ridicule of the community? Today we thank God that Joseph obeyed God. In this courage he is a great demonstration of the grace of God. He is a worthy example.

11

FROM THE MANGER TO THE CROSS

From the manger to the Cross – a span of about thirty years.

From the manger to the Cross – one event spiritually.

Christ was not given for the beauty of babyhood or for the glory of the virgin birth,

Nor was He given for the beauty of an exemplary life..

He was given to the Crucifixion.

The shadow of the Cross falls across the manger.

The shaft of light from the star of Bethlehem points to the Child born crucified.

It is most fitting that we should go to Calvary at Christmas.

12

THE NEW YEAR

Predictions abound as we enter a new year. Radio, television, and the printed media are telling us of economic uncertainty, the possibility of war (in fact, in this modern world there is always war somewhere), the break up of the 'traditional family', and the loss of traditional values. These predictions come out of worldly thinking. As the world offers us this kind of intimidation, it also offers us its own cures. The problem is that the cures come out of the same source as the diagnosis.

These cures revolve around such things as materialism, personal aggression, and a host of worldly philosophies. Common to these cures are such expressions as 'be your own best friend', 'look out for number one', 'master the art of one upmanship', and many other clichés of worldly wisdom. Though couched in the form of aggression and boldness, they represent the spirit of fear. We cannot face the New Year with this kind of intimidation.

'God has not given us the spirit of fear; but of power, and of love, and of a sound mind' (1 Timothy 1.7). The power promised here is a confidence based on the sovereignty of God. It is confidence drawn from the trustworthiness of the word of God and imparted by the Spirit of God. The second defense that God has given us is the Spirit of love – the Holy Spirit. The world is afraid to love; it is afraid of the risks involved in love.

In Christ love and power are united, and they are pure. Love does not dilute true power by sentimentality, and it is not trampled by misguided powerfulness. This is the Spirit of a sound mind, self control, sober mindedness, and discipline. These qualities are essential to confident living.

'But the wisdom which is from above is first pure, then peaceable, gentle, and easy to be entreated, full of mercy and good fruits, without partiality, and without hypocrisy. And the fruit of righteousness is sown in peace of them that make peace' (James 3.17, 18).

13

HUMAN MERIT

(Did I say, 'Merit'? That's a Laugh!)

What is the biblical evaluation of human merit? Of human knowledge, the Scriptures speak of foolishness. Of human strength, the Scriptures speak of weakness. Of human righteousness, the Scriptures speak of filthy rags. Of the significance of humankind, the Scriptures ask, 'What is man, that thou art mindful of him? And the son of man, that thou visitest him?' (Psalm 8.4).

By precept and historical example the Scriptures show up human frailty: frailty of body, so that individuals may be swept into death at any moment; frailty of moral stamina, so that men and women are overcome with moral filth on impulse; frailty of soul and spirit, so that people fall into sin under the most foolish of temptations. The biblical narrative abounds with illustrations of this truth: Israel as a nation, Abraham, Samson, David, Solomon, and many other individuals.

The sum of this truth is that a vain self trust – and all self trust is vain – is the inception of sin. Observe Peter's boast, 'Though all men shall be offended because of thee, yet will I never be offended' (Matthew 26.33). It is sinful because it will not hear the warning of the word of God. It is sinful because it will not plead the grace of God. It is sinful because it will not hear divine wisdom. 'Wherefore let him that thinketh he standeth take heed lest he fall' (2 Corinthians 10.12).

14

PRAY FOR OUR PRESIDENT (WHOEVER HE OR SHE IS)

Special note. The following article was written on the occasion of the inaugural of President Ronald Reagan. Particulars are passing things, but the message is unchanged from one president to another.

'I exhort therefore, that first of all, supplications, prayers, intercessions and giving of thanks be made for all men: for kings, and for all that are in authority; that we may lead a quiet and peaceable life in all godliness and honesty' (1 Timothy 2.1, 2).

In a republic such as our own it is easy for us to become so taken up with the political process that we let ourselves neglect the most important political service that we as believers in Christ can ever render: prayer for those in authority. President Jimmy Carter has come through a difficult period in the history of the United States. How many of us berated him when we should have prayed for him?

President Carter is in special need of our prayers now. He has faced and is going through a traumatic personal crisis. He is attempting to resolve the hostage crisis – United States armed forces personnel being held captive by an enemy nation – within the closing days of his administration. He is passing the reigns of government to his successor with dignity. By his testimony he is our brother in Christ. Let us pray for him.

President-elect Reagan is also in special need of our prayers. He takes the helm of government at a difficult time. He faces inflation, unemployment problems, international leadership problems, and perhaps a lingering hostage problem.

Tuesday, January 20, 1981 is inauguration day. Quite properly it will be a day of festivity. However, it should also be a day of sobriety and prayer. Let us spend some special period of time on Tuesday in prayer for our government and those who lead it. The exiles at the time of the 'seventy years captivity' were exhorted, 'And seek the peace of the city whither I have caused you to be carried away captives, and pray unto the Lord for it: for in peace thereof shall have peace' (Jeremiah 29.7). If God called on Israel to seek the peace of the cities of their captivity, He certainly calls on us to seek the peace of our nation. In seeking peace we find peace.

15

How to Cultivate Faith

The promises of God are not fulfilled by repeating the promises as if they were some kind of mantra designed to coax God into compliance with our wishes. It is not what we say that determines what we receive. It is what God says that determines what we receive.

So the essential question is, 'How is faith cultivated?' Faith must have a proper (that is, a biblical) understanding of God. Note Abraham's example. He looked on God as the One who is able to make the dead live, and to call into existence things that do not exist (Romans 4.17). Abraham's God was all-powerful, and all powers were subject to Him. It is not a question of how strong is your faith. How strong is mustard seed (Matthew 17.20; Luke 17.6)? It is a question of how strong is your God.

Abraham's example also teaches us how to claim the promises of God. Abraham set aside the lack of hope from a natural standpoint, and believed in hope on the ground of the promise of God. He recognized the fact of his own body 'now dead' and the 'deadness of Sarah's womb'. Above all of that he recognized the superseding fact of the life giving power of the word of God (Romans 4.19).

How does one cultivate this faith? Not simply by repetition of promises or by repetition of prayers, but by feeding on the word of God. 'So then faith cometh by hearing, and hearing by the word of God' (Romans 10.17). Faith is born of the Word. It is nurtured by the

Word. If you would be strong, be strong in the word of God.

16

WHAT MAKES A PERSON SIGNIFICANT?

In the presence of Christ people are measured in terms of their need and not in terms of their station in life. The people of nobility and powerful station in life who came before Christ were in the same category as the poor, powerless, and despised. In the courts of humanity the great ones have preference. In the court of Christ the children, the powerless, the diseased, the sinful have position and grace. All are measured in the light of two facts: the holiness of God and the sinfulness of humankind. All are acceptable in the light of one fact: the grace of God in Christ.

So we do not remember those who came in contact with Christ because of their station in life whether that station was one of nobility or one of dereliction. We remember them because of their encounter with our Lord. Except for Him they are not memorable.

Some of these people went away from their encounter with Jesus damned. Herod, Pilate, the rich young ruler, and many others. Some went away saved: the Syro-Phoenician woman, the woman taken in adultery, the Samaritan woman, Nicodemus, and many others. Whatever was the outcome of their meeting with Christ, the fact for which these people find a place in history is that they met Jesus.

Upon this Man and upon such meetings the issues of time and eternity hinge. We also have our meeting with the Son of God, and this fact gives us significance.

'What is man that thou art mindful of him? And the son of man that thou visitest him?' (Psalm 8.4).

17

BE ANXIOUS FOR NOTHING

'Therefore take no thought saying, What shall we eat? Or what shall we drink? or wherewithal shall we be clothed?' (Matthew 6.31).

How will I be clothed? Where is the next meal coming from? These are not questions that should create anxiety in the believer, 'For after all these things the gentiles seek ...' (Matthew 6.32). Jesus has explained this. No amount of thinking about it can produce a larger body; no anxiety can make one taller. This is an insignificant thing; yet we try to settle the great issues of life by anxiety.

God clothes the flower of the field with a beauty that is greater than Solomon's clothing. Compared with the issues of life and death, lilies are insignificant, but God adorns them. They are beautiful without striving. Will not our heavenly Father provide for us in the same way?

Living is not a thing to be striven after. Clothing is not a thing to be covetous about. God has given life; He has fixed and He provides the principles for the sustenance of life. Striving is not one of those principles, and it cannot alter God's provisions.

Anxiety, worry, and fretting over food and clothing are futile and faithless. God is Ruler over life and all the provision of life. God knows that we need these things. Let us spend our energies in seeking the kingdom of God and His righteousness (Matthew 6.33).

18

WHAT IS PRAYER?

What is prayer? It is honest talk with God, with emphasis on honest. It is our speech to God and our waiting to hear what He has to say to us. In other words, it is communion – conversation with God.

The psalms reveal this aspect of prayer in many ways. They discuss with God every human emotion and circumstance. They do not hide or excuse their thoughts of anger and vengeance. They do not hide their weaknesses. They even speak to God about their doubts – doubts about the reward of righteousness and about the course of divine providence. They confess their sins openly to God. They call sin 'sin' and do not gloss it over with silly words like mistake, misunderstanding, etc. They do not excuse it by saying, 'I am just a human being,' or 'I just did what is natural'.

These same writers record God's answers to their prayers. Sometimes God grants their petitions. Sometimes He corrects and rebukes their thoughts. He also comforts them in their weaknesses, both physical and spiritual. He forgives their sins, but however God responds, there is always a worship response on the part of the psalmist.

The point is that prayer opens the whole person to God. It is not a dress parade of the things we want to be or think we are. It is not our self-recommendations to God. It is communion with God as we are, with confession of sins, praise for mercy, thanksgiving for the ways of God's providence, and petition for further answers from God. There is no human need that is not a proper petition before our Father. Prayer is the whole person bared to God without any attempt to be what we are not.

Prayer is also our waiting to hear what God has to say to us. God speaks to us in many ways: most specifically and frequently out of His written Word. However, God speaks to us through the guidance of the Holy Spirit, by words of wisdom, knowledge, prophecy, interpretation, and discernment.

Do we wait to hear what God has to say? If we do not, prayer is not complete.

19

HOLINESS AND CHRIST'S RETURN

On television, on radio, from many pulpits, and in the printed medium one hears a great deal about the return of our Lord. We get 'psyched up' about it and about what the world is going to be like when the Lord returns. We fantasize about how it will feel as we 'fly through the air' to meet Him. These things do not constitute spiritual expectancy.

Spiritual expectancy can be shown predominantly in only one way – a life of holiness. Hear the words of John, 'Beloved, now are we the sons of God, and it doth not yet appear what we shall be: but we know that, when he shall appear, we shall be like him; for we shall see him as he is. And everyone that hath this hope in him [that is, in Jesus] purifieth himself even as he is pure' (1 John 3.2, 3).

The holiness of which the Scriptures speak is both a specific experience provided in the atonement and it is a way of life. The perspective of that holiness is the coming again of Jesus. 'And the very God of peace sanctify you wholly; and I pray God your whole spirit and soul and body be preserved blameless unto the coming of our Lord Jesus Christ' (1 Thessalonians 5.23).

The apostles in the New Testament preached the doctrine of holiness and practices of pure living hand in hand with the doctrine of the second coming. These two doctrines are bound together in the teachings of Jesus (John 17), in the preaching in the book of Acts, and in the epistles of the New Testament. Pentecost is the fruit of holiness, and it is witness to Jesus' return. If Pentecost does not always have these two perspectives, it will lose its vigor and ultimately its identity. Pentecostalism would then be just another 'ism,' existing in name only with no real evidence of the power of the Holy Spirit.

What shall we do about this? Let the blood of Christ cleanse us from all unrighteousness. Let the word of God convict and correct us. Let the graces of Christ abound in us that we do not become barren and unfruitful (1 Peter 1.1-11). Let the Holy Spirit quicken us to the prayer, 'Even so, come, Lord Jesus' (Revelation 22.20).

20

WHAT IS THE MEASURE OF GREATNESS?

The measure of a person is the magnitude of his/her service to God and others, and the extent of self-sacrifice. The extent to which a person reserves himself/herself for himself/herself is the degree to which that person stunts personal growth and spiritual stature. This measure, and this measure alone, determines greatness or smallness of and individual. The fact that a person is rejected by others or that his/her gifts are spurned, or even abused, does not affect stature.

Herein is the greatness of the Son of Man. As a man He was perfect morally and spiritually, and He manifested His perfection by His expenditure of Himself for others, even His enemies. He did not seek greatness by becoming a servant; because He was great He became a servant. He did not give Himself as a ransom for many in order to become great. He is great – infinitely so; so, He gave His life a ransom for many (Philippians 2.5-11; Matthew 20.28; Mark 10.45; 1 Timothy 2.5, 6).

He gave Himself as no other man before or since. His life, which was His and not ours, He gave in order to redeem our lives which we had forfeited. Because He was great He was able to pay the ransom to buy back our lives. He was great enough to pay the forfeiture. He was also great enough to be willing to pay the price for our salvation (Hebrews 2.3. 4).

The place of His great sacrifice was the Cross; the place of our great sacrifice is also the Cross. Through the Cross, we become the servants of others for Christ's sake. 'For we preach not ourselves, but Christ Jesus the Lord; and ourselves your servants for Jesus' sake' (2 Corinthians 4.5).

21

JESUS PASSED BY

Jesus moved with determined purpose from the Mount of Transfiguration to Mount Calvary. 'And it came to pass, when the time was come that he should be received up, he steadfastly set his face to go to Jerusalem' (Luke 9.51). He moved in the fulfillment of His Father's will. Along the way, he did marvelous things.

His disciples went ahead of Him, preached the kingdom of God, healed the sick, and cast out devils. He visited Mary and Martha gracing their home with divine presence. He taught the disciples to pray (Luke 11.1-4). He healed the crippled woman. He healed the man of dropsy. He cleansed ten lepers at one time. He blessed the little children that some would have barred from His presence. He talked with the rich young ruler who was very near the kingdom of God. He healed blind Bartimaeus and saved the publican Zacchaeus. All the while He taught His followers many things about Himself and the kingdom of God – all of this as He made His way to crucifixion.

Marvin P. Dalton caught the spirit of this in a gospel song entitled 'Jesus Passed By'. Hear the words.

> There is a story of long ago,
> Man roamed in darkness nowhere to go;
> One day the scene changed, they ceased to cry,
> There was a reason Jesus passed by.
>
> Man found compassion, hungry were fed,
> Some saw their loved ones raised from the dead;

They found great comfort came from on high.
There was a reason Jesus passed by.

One day a sinner, I found relief,
Gone was my burden, gone was my grief;
Angels were singing, and so was I,
There was a reason, Jesus passed by.'[1]

Though our Lord has now been crucified, has arisen from the dead, and ascended to His Father's side, He is still passing by. His presence has the same effect today that it had then. The sick are healed; the blind see; the dead are raised; sins are forgiven, and the poor have the gospel preached to them.

Jesus is still passing by.

---

[1] Used by permission

22

FATHER, FORGIVE THEM

'Father, forgive them' is the watchword of Christian love. It became so when our Lord spoke these words from the Cross. It is in forgiving that He died; it is in forgiving that we live.

From the vantage point of Mount Calvary Jesus saw all of time and all people. All those whom He saw He prayed for. He looked back to Adam and Eve in their first sin. He saw Cain as the first murderer. He saw the centuries long parade of Old Testament believers who had passed by the Holy of Holies, where the priests ministered on their behalf.

Of those in His own days on earth He saw all those who had despitefully used Him. Herod who would have slain Him as an infant; the insincere crowd who had welcomed Him to Jerusalem; the Jewish leaders who had condemned Him and demanded His death; Pilate who had allowed His crucifixion; Barabbas who had been exchanged for Him; the two thieves who were dying with Him; and the Roman soldiers who had nailed Him to the Tree.

Among the disciples He saw Peter who had denied Him, Judas who had betrayed Him, Joseph of Arimathea and Nicodemus who were afraid to profess Him openly, and the disciples who followed Him afar off.

From this vantage point of His glory Jesus also looked to the end of the age. He saw all the people who would ever be, and He saw those struggling under the burden of sin and plagued by the ravages of hatred, disease, and death. He saw sinners of every sort and in every depth of sin.

For all those whom we have mentioned He prayed, 'Father, forgive them'. Surely in this list you have seen yourself, as I have seen myself. This prayer is for you and me, and Jesus is today at the Father's right hand praying again and again, 'Father, forgive them'. He lives forever to make intercession for all those who come to God by Him (Hebrews 7.25).

23

CHRIST IS RISEN

The Cross of Christ gives us a picture of the deepest and most sublime love the world has ever known. It is a demonstration of the Father's love in that He gave His Son (John 3.16; Romans 5.6-11). It is a demonstration of the Son's love in that He gave His life (John 15.13). It is a demonstration of the grace of God in that this was done for an undeserving world.

Regardless of the nobility of His death, the dying of Jesus cannot meet the needs of humankind. A dead Jesus cannot justify, cannot give life and cannot reign; He 'was delivered for our offences, and was raised again for our justification' (Romans 4.25).

Jesus' death is unique; He reigned in His dying. He laid down His life that He might take it up again. In the manner of His dying He provided for His own resurrection. 'No man taketh it [i.e. His life] from me, but I lay it down of myself. I have power to lay it down, and I have power to take it again. This commandment have I received of my Father' (John 10.18).

Herein is the uniqueness of the Christian faith. No other religion celebrated or believes in the bodily resurrection of its founder.

Go to the tomb of Gautama Buddha, and his follower say, 'There he lies'.

Go to the tomb of Confucius and his followers say, 'There he lies'.

Go to the tomb of Mohamed and his followers say, 'There he lies'.

Go to the tomb of Jesus and His followers say, 'There He lay! Why seek ye the living among the dead?'

HALLELJUH! CHRIST IS RISEN

HE IS RISEN, INDEED!

24

WHAT DOES THE RESURRECTION OF CHRIST MEAN FOR US?

Place yourself in the mind of the early disciples. You are now convinced that Jesus has been raised from the dead. You have heard the reports, and perhaps by this time, you have even seen the resurrected Jesus.

You have to ask yourself, 'What does all this mean?' Does it mean that Jesus will immediately restore the kingdom to Israel? Does it mean that Jesus will go to Jerusalem, purify the temple once again, and sit on His throne in the holy city? Does it mean that the law of the Lord will become the law of the entire earth? Does it mean that I will not have to die? These and many other questions would run through your mind, but where would you get the answers?

God did give the answers, but He gave them over years of revelation, especially as it is recorded in the New Testament. The following is a summary of those answers.

In His resurrection and ascension Christ was exalted above all (Ephesians 1.20-23). He is exalted in order that every knee should bow and every tongue should confess that He is Lord (Philippians 2.9, 10). By His resurrection He was declared to the Son of God in power by the Spirit of holiness (Romans 1.4). By His resurrection He accomplished our justification (Romans 4.25). By His resurrection life we are born again and follow Him in newness of life (Ephesians 2.1; Romans 6.8-11). By His resurrection and ascension He has received gifts for those who believe on Him. The chief of these gifts is that He has received the Promise of the Father – the Holy Spirit – and He has poured out that Spirit upon believers (Acts 2.1-4, 32, 34; Ephesians 4.8-12). By His resurrection he is the Source and guarantee of our resurrection. He has shown us the nature of our resurrection (1 Corinthians 15.20-28). By His resurrection He has conquered death thus breaking the bondage of the law, robbing the grave of its victory, and removing the sting of death (1 Corinthians 15.54-58).

25

RIGHT IS NOT MIGHT (BUT IT WILL PULL DOWN STRONGHOLDS!)

Peter tried to defend the Lord with a sword, and he made a mess of things. In politics we would call it a 'debacle'. The Lord had to intervene; He healed the high priest's servant, and told Peter to put up his sword. Peter attempted to fight a spiritual battle with a carnal weapon.

Today a great many causes are being defended and supported by carnal weapons. Many of these causes have become political issues: prayer in the schools, right to life, racial justice, fair employment practices, the rights of the poor and minorities, freedom from sexual harassment, protection of children from abuse, and many others.

We must not draw back from the support of any right cause, but we must be prayerful and careful in how we defend and support these causes. Right cannot be defended by character assassination of our opponents. It is no glory to God when being born again is traded in the market place to gain votes. Righteous conclusions cannot be defended by claims that are not true, but twisted statistics and unsupportable theories. Godliness cannot reign in our lives and in our nation when we allow angry demonstrations which rob others of their rights in order to gain political clout.

Hatred of an evil cannot include hatred of the evildoer. The right to worship cannot include the violation of the rights of the non-worshiper. Evangelism does not include the right to belittle and humiliate any unbeliever.

If any would ask, what are we to do, our answer is in the words of Jesus. 'Therefore all things whatsoever ye would that men should do to you, do ye even so to them: for this is the law and the prophets' (Matthew 7.12). This is the way to treat your family, your friends, even your enemies.

26

MOTHER'S DAY

Motherhood has been greatly romanticized, and this has created an image of mothers that no woman can fulfill – the always calm, always beautiful, always wise, always indulgent, always perfect 'pal' to her children, always busy in the home, always busy outside the home, always relaxed, always perfectly dressed for every occasion, always ... always ... always ... ad infinitum ... ad nauseam.

What is wrong with this picture? First it creates an impossible and undesirable ideal – an ideal that creates frustration and self condemnation when one fails to equal this fictional goddess. Second, it creates false views of the family, as if mothers are indestructible and incapable of the hurts and loneliness that her children and husband experience. Third, it creates the kind of presumption that lets us give mother one day a year for 364 days of harassment and being taken for granted. Leap year is even worse by one additional day. Fourth, and most important, it ignores the necessity of the grace of God in the proper experience of motherhood.

The biblical view of the mother is an exalted view: Eve the mother of all living, Sarah the mother of the child of promise, the mother of King Lemuel who taught him prophecy, Mary the mother of Jesus, Lois and Eunice who taught Timothy the word of God, and many others.

Besides these specific examples there are many figures of speech in Scripture that depict an exalted view of motherhood. Wisdom is described in the image of motherhood. The fruitful and redeemed Israel is shown in the image of motherhood. The heavenly Jerusalem is called the mother of us all.

The one common ground of all these examples is the grace of God. Eve was designated the mother of all living after her grievous sin. Sarah bore Isaac after her lapse of faith that produced Ishmael by her handmaid Hagar. The announcement to Mary that she would give birth to the Messiah designated her as 'favored in the grace of God'.

It is the grace of God that has exalted motherhood and given it beauty. Motherhood is an experience in worship and faith. It is an experience in the grace of God.

27

THE COURAGE OF THE OBEDIENCE OF FAITH

'Be strong and of good courage; be not afraid, neither be thou dismayed: for the Lord thy God is with thee whithersoever thou goest' (Joshua 1.9).

Joshua and Israel were on the threshold of Canaan when God spoke these words to them. Moses had died; Israel now faces a new task under a new leader Joshua. God encouraged them with this exhortation.

The exhortation to be strong and courageous involves the moral courage of faith. Moral courage is essential if one is to do the will of God. God specified this in Joshua 1.7, 'Only be thou strong and very courageous, that thou mayest observe to do according to all the law, which Moses my servant commanded you ...' To obey God is the supreme test of moral courage. Obedience is holiness; it is the strictness of life that turns not from the law of God to the right hand or to the left. This courage comes by the grace of God.

Living by faith is also an act of courage. The Apostle Paul combines obedience and faith in his phrase the 'obedience of faith' (Romans 1.5; 16.26). In Israel's case the land of promise lay before them. It was a vast territory and it was occupied by powerful enemies – enemies that would not willingly give up the land. These are all reasons for fear from the natural point of view. However in this case God had promised the land to His people Israel, and He had promised to fight the battles for Israel. He had also promised, 'For the Lord thy God is with you whithersoever thou goest'. Wherever the Israelites would set their feet, they had the promise of the presence of God. This promise included the most remote sections of the land and the most difficult battle sites.

This exhortation and promise were given to Israel under a specific circumstance. The same promise comes to us today. The issue of moral courage to live a holy life is still the same. The issue of the courage to take God's promises as the basis of our actions and as the ground for living is still the same. 'Thus saith the Lord unto you, Be not afraid nor dismayed by reason of this great multitude: for the battle is not yours but God's' (2 Chronicles 20.15b).

28

GOD IN THE HANDS OF AN ANGRY SINNER

Jonathan Edwards, a powerful preacher of early New England days, preached a sermon entitled 'Sinners in the Hand of an Angry God'. It is said that people held onto the pews for fear that they would fall into the flames of hell. Some people today would call that 'graveyard story' preaching, or would accuse the preacher of trying to scare people into salvation.

So angry, sinful people have 'taken hold' of God and attempted to do with God the things that put them at ease. Perhaps we should recruit this ancient and famous sermon with the title 'God in the Hands of an Angry Sinner'. Look at what humanity has done to God.

Humanists want a religion without God. So people create various substitutes for God: the nobility of the human race, the infinite perfectibility of humankind, scientism, the power behind the universe, the unity of all things, peace, love, and many other silly nothings.

What are the results of such thinking? Here are some of them. Humankind elevates its own pleasure, physical comfort, bodily health, longevity, medically produced 'immortality', material wealth, the good life, the beautiful people, and many other human ambitions. These are treated as if they are divine promises, or perhaps we should call them divine aspirations. Humankind elevates itself to the level of God by claiming to be 'captain' of his soul and 'master' of his fate. Scientific powers are elevated to the level of controlling life, claiming the power to create life. The power to do a thing is then conceived as the mandate to do it. If this 'god' can create life, it can destroy life. This also becomes divine command, after all we can't leave our mistakes around to litter the environment. That could be embarrassing.

This kind of person – the modern 'god maker' – will not tolerate the biblical revelation of God seen in the face of Jesus Christ, the 'brightness of His glory and the express image of his person' (Hebrews 1.3). So he or she remakes Christ in his or her own image. The god thus made becomes the image and servant of his or her creator. He serves human needs, approves human value systems and ambitions, and gives him or her pleasure.

Perhaps the Apostle Paul would say to modern humanity (on a late night 'Larry King Live' episode), the same thing he said on Mars Hill, 'I perceive that in all things ye are too superstitious' (Acts 17.22).

All human-made religions are superstition!

29

PRAYER AS MORAL DUTY AND PRIVILEGE

All things are open to the eyes of God. We cannot reveal anything to Him that He does not already know and has known from eternity. The longing in our hearts for communion and love, the needs both physical and spiritual that we have, the sins that we have committed, the hurts that we hide from each other. 'All things are naked and opened unto the eyes of him with whom we have to do' (Hebrews 4.13).

Some may ask, 'Why pray if God already knows?' First, prayer is moral obligation. We like to think of it as privilege, and it is. But the human person cannot be fully realized without communion with God, who is the Origin of human nature and personhood. God requires people to fulfill their humanness and purpose of existence. There will be no rest until humanity returns to its origin.

Second, it is a valuable spiritual experience for us to open up to God. In the confession of sins we expose ourselves to the judgment and the forgiveness of God. In making our requests we lay bare the desires of our hearts to the loving heavenly Father. In telling God about the frustrations of our lives we cast our burdens upon Christ's Cross where they have already been resolved. In praise we offer to God the 'sacrifice of praise … the fruit of our lips' (Hebrews 13.15).

We offer all worship through the high Priest who understands all the problems and temptations that we have. 'for we have not an high priest which cannot be touched with the feeling of our infirmities; but was in all points tempted like as we are, yet without sin' (Hebrews 4.15). He invites us to come boldly (that is, with complete assurance of acceptance) before the throne of grace. 'Let us therefore come boldly unto the throne of grace, that we may obtain mercy, and find grace to help in time of need' (Hebrews 4.16). The One who sits on this throne is the King of grace.

If this were a throne of rewards for righteousness, we would be intimidated. We might well question, 'Have I paid the price to be here?' That is not our question. We have only three questions. First, has Christ paid the price? Second, has God made the promise? Third, has the Holy Spirit cried in us, 'Abba, Father'? The answer to all is 'Yes!' In that case we may come boldly to the throne of grace.

30

TO SEE THE BEST AND ACCEPT THE SECOND BEST

A Korean proverb completes the sentence above. 'To see the best and accept the second best is the beginning of spiritual decay.' This is a profound spiritual truth. The first thing to observe about this statement is what it does not say. It does not say, 'To see the best and choose the second best ...' Simply the acceptance of the second best – a passive acceptance of second best options – is the beginning of spiritual decay.

We must apply this principle to all areas of life and living: social, political, domestic, industrial, and religious. To accept second best options breaks down the basic principle of faithfulness. This is where compromise first appears. It does not start in bold and flagrant violations of faithfulness and spirituality. The seed of flagrant violations is present in the mere acceptance of second best.

To accept the second best robs God of what is rightfully His. We are His; He has purchased our best by giving His Best, the only begotten Son. We who have been purchased with so great a price cannot afford paltry second best choices to be offered in the worship of the God of infinite love.

This is the principle of faithfulness in small things, for the truly great things are simply the accumulation of many small things into one. Life that is built on a series of second best choices cannot total anything but a second best life. A life that is built on seeing the best and choosing the best is a life of faithfulness and true greatness in God's sight. Notice the change in the verb; the best is never a mere passive acquiescence. This is a determination to offer to God the sacrifice of our lives. 'But to do good and give of yourselves do not neglect, for with such sacrifices God is well pleased' (Hebrews 13.16).

The Apostle Paul sums up this entire idea in a very positive statement. 'Finally, my brethren, whatsoever things are true, whatsoever things are honest, whatsoever things are just, whatsoever things pure, whatsoever things are lovely, whatsoever things are of good report; if there be any virtue, and if there be any praise, think on these things' (Philippians 4.8).

31

YOU ARE THE EPISTLE OF CHRIST

Hearts of stone have been transformed into hearts of flesh by the grace of the new birth. The old heart of stone could not receive the inscription of Christ's message. That heart was too brittle and it was lifeless; only condemnation and hardness could be written on such a tablet.

By the new birth God has made a new heart – a new tablet for the inscription of a new commandment of love (1 John 2.8-11). On this new tablet the message of Christ's love, peace, and reconciliation can by written by the Holy Spirit. As the 'finger of God' He wrote the Ten Commandments on stone tablets for the nation of Israel. As the 'Finger of God' He writes the new commandment of love on every believing heart. 'And this is his commandment, That we should believe in the name of his Son Jesus Christ, and love one another, as he gave us commandment' (1 John 3.23).

Now the question is, 'How well have we allowed the Holy Spirit to write Christ's message on our hearts?' Do we still carry some of the old message that was more appropriate to the heart of stone than to the heart of flesh? What does the world see when they see our attitudes, hear our conversations, and watch our works? Is the message on our hearts and read by the world the message of love, joy, peace, brotherly kindness, patience, mercy, and longsuffering? This is the message that Christ would write on our hearts by the Holy Spirit. Forasmuch as ye are manifestly declared to be the epistle of Christ ministered by us, written not with ink, but with the Spirit of the living God; not in tables of stone, but in the fleshly tables of the heart' (2 Corinthians 3.3).

32

YOU CAN'T BOX WITH GOD

A number of years ago a play was featured in theatres especially in the northeastern United States entitled, 'You can't box with God. Your arms are too short.' You say, 'This is obvious'. Of course it is, but how many times have we attempted to escape the consequences of our sins? Isn't that an attempt to 'box' with God?

We neglect church attendance and expect God to be as indulgent with us as we are with ourselves. We neglect to pray and expect to continue to be strong spiritually. We don't read the word of God and expect to have strong faith. We bite and devour one another and don't expect to be consumed one by another. We let our standard of holy living slip and think that we can and will stop with only a 'little compromise'. We expect our friendship with the world to go unnoticed by God. We seem to think that we can neglect the stewardship of our tithes and offerings and God will bless in our hands what is rightfully His.

There are at least three things wrong with this kind of thinking. First, we ignore the practices of good spiritual health. We cannot neglect the practices of good health physically without inviting disease. Second, we disregard the spiritual well being of our brothers and sisters in Christ's body by weakening the body of Christ by our own compromises, prayerlessness, lack of feeding on the Word, and sacrificeless living. Third, we forget that God says, 'Be not deceived; God is not mocked. For whatsoever a man soweth, that shall he also reap' (Galatians 6.7).

We may ignore God's existence, but He will not ignore our neglect of Him. We may forget the laws of God, but He does not forget whether we have obeyed them.

You can't box with God; your arms are too short. But your can walk with God and know that He does not forget that either. 'He that soweth to the Spirit shall of the Spirit reap life everlasting' (Galatians 6.8b). Give up the struggle and walk in the Spirit. We can be free in Christ's yoke, and rest under His burden (Matthew 11.30).

33

Proclaim Liberty

The story is told that an old bellman had been in the steeple of the Philadelphia State House (later designated as Independence Hall) since the delegates (from the colonies) gathered in the morning; he was waiting for a signal from a boy stationed at the door below. On the bell in this steeple was the inscription from Leviticus 'Proclaim liberty throughout the land unto all the inhabitants thereof'. A declaration of liberty was expected from the patriots who were gathered there, and the old man hastened to proclaim it when the boy below clapped his hands and shouted, 'Ring! Ring!' This was the signal for the birth of the Republic dedicated to the freedom of the human spirit and destined to power beyond man's dreams.[2]

That proclamation of liberty was issued in the midst of conflict, and a conflict of doubtful outcome. It was a proclamation that was meaningless and a liability unless the battle continued and resulted in victory for the American patriots. Those who signed that declaration signed the forfeiture of their own properties; they signed their own death warrants if the battle was not won by the patriots.

Jesus invites you to hear a proclamation of liberty that has no such liabilities.

---

[2] Dumas Malone, **The Story of the Declaration of Independence** (New York. Oxford University Press, 1975), p. 3

The Spirit of the Lord is upon me, because he has anointed me to preach the gospel to the poor; He has sent me under commission to preach freedom to the captives and sight to the blind, to send the shattered ones out in freedom and to preach the acceptable year of the Lord (Luke 4.18, 19).

When the Son of Man descends from heaven with the shout of triumph and with the voice of the arch angel liberty will be proclaimed anew. It is a liberty with no doubtful outcome, and whose victory has already been won. The victory was accomplished at the Cross and was fulfilled in the resurrection. Now we proclaim liberty to the captives and the opening of prison doors. 'On behalf of Christ, we are acting as ambassadors while God is urging through us, We beseech you on the behalf of Christ, Be ye reconciled to God' (2 Corinthians 5.20).

34

WE HAVE FOUND THE MESSIAH

Devout Israelites lived in the hope of the appearance of the Messiah. He would fulfill the Scripture promises and would bring in the kingdom of God.

Prophets in Israel had promised, 'He is coming'. The pinnacle of the prophecies would be the announcement saying, 'He has come'. John the Baptist had that privilege. Standing at the summit of all Old Testament prophets, he proclaimed, 'Behold the Lamb of God, which taketh away the sin of the world' (John 1.29). He was able to follow through in his preaching and say, 'The kingdom of God is at hand' (Mark 1.14, 15).

The coming of the King and His kingdom calls for heralds who will proclaim the coming of the King. John was that herald in the days of our Lord's presence among us in the flesh. Prior to His ascension, Jesus promised to return, and He commissioned His disciples to be witnesses in the power of the Holy Spirit 'both in Jerusalem and in all Judaea, and in Samaria, and unto the uttermost part of the earth [until the end of the age]' (Acts 1.8; Matthew 28.19, 20). The prospect of Christ's second appearance calls for new heralds of His coming.

There is an important spiritual function here. It is the obligation of those who have found the Messiah to tell others that He has come. This obligation is twofold. First we have an obligation to the Messiah Himself to let it be known that He has come and that He is coming again. It is His will that we tell of His coming.

Second, we have an obligation to those who do not know and have not heard. Those who have the gospel have a moral debt to those who do not have it. Would we not feel obligated to tell people that a forest fire was racing toward their homes if they did not know it? This obligation is infinitely greater, because we have the privilege of announcing the King of kings and saving men and women from hell. The Apostle Paul put it this way, 'I am a debtor both to the Greeks and to the Barbarians, both to the wise and the unwise. So as much as in me is, I am ready to preach the gospel to you that are at Rome also' (Romans 1.14, 15)

35

GOD IS FAITHFUL

It is not my hold on God's hand or my determination to be saved that will save me. It is His hold on my hand and His determination for me to be saved that will save me. The glory of Christian living is not the stamina of believers but the strength and faithfulness of our heavenly Father.

Yet I cannot allow myself to be presumptuous on God's grace. The faithfulness of God and the obligation of the believer to be faithful are brought together in the words of Philippians 2.12, 13. First, Paul reminds the Philippians of their obligation to be faithful in the obedience of faith. 'Wherefore, my beloved, as ye have always obeyed, not as in my presence only, but now much more in my absence, work out your own salvation in fear and trembling.' In this effort we do not struggle alone, 'For it is God which worketh in you both to will and to do of His good pleasure'.

Even in temptation God's promise is that He will make a way of escape within the temptation itself. God's faithfulness controls our temptations. He will not permit a temptation that does not have a way out of the temptation. He knows the one who is being tempted; he knows the strength of that person. Beyond these considerations God does not permit temptation. There is no irresistible temptation.

God does not spare us temptation. He did not shield the first man and woman from temptation (Genesis 3.1-7). He did not even spare His own Son temptation (Mark

1.12, 13; Luke 4.1-13). When Jesus returned from the wilderness of temptation, He 'returned in the power of the Spirit into Galilee' (Luke 4.14).

There is no strength in 'hot house Christians'. God allows temptation, but under circumstances in which He personally makes a way of escape. When we face temptation, we may know that it is not our duty to make a way of escape; God has promised to do that. 'There hath no temptation taken you but such as is common to man: but God is faithful, who will not suffer you to be tempted above that ye are able; but will with the temptation make a way to escape, that ye may be able to bear it' (1 Corinthians 10.13). Even though the believer may be pressed by temptation of the most severe sort, he or she can trust God to deliver.

36

WHAT BELONGS TO GOD? EVERYTHING AND EVERYONE
WHAT BELONGS TO CAESAR? NOTHING; IT ALL BELONGS TO GOD

'Render to Caesar the things that are Caesar's and to God the things that are God's' (Mark 12.17). Christ, in this statement, is teaching neither union of church and state nor separation of church and state. We are the ones who impose that politicized issue on this statement. Christ was teaching that duty to both God and government are issues of morality and spirituality.

Christians (born again; there is no such thing as a non-born again Christian) cannot divorce responsibilities to the state from his or her commitment to God. The Christian voter must seek the guidance of the Holy Spirit and the tests of the word of God in political activity and especially in voting. Christians who are elected and appointed officials (and there are many: legislators, governors, mayors, council members, heads of government bureaus, etc.) must sponsor and support or oppose government policy (including legislation and directives) according to the standards of righteousness in Scripture. Christian law enforcement officials (from Attorneys General to the officer on the beat) must consider the fact that they are the ministers of God (Romans 13.4). They serve under His ordination (Romans 13.1). The application and enforcement of the law must be by the word of God and in the Spirit of holiness and love.

Christian citizens must follow the Bible in their submission and obedience.

This is not union of church and state, but it does give the government the strongest possible support by the church and its constituents. This is as it should be because civil government is ordained by God (Romans 13.1-8; 1 Timothy 2.1-4). Support – especially in prayer – is obedience to God, as He exhorts in His Word.

The church and individual members of the church will at times find it necessary to oppose some legislation, government directives, judicial decrees, and practices of enforcement. At times the church may be morally compelled to speak out against a candidate or government official because of his or her record in moral issues and practices. This is not an opposition to the state; neither is it disobedience to the state. It is, in fact, loyalty to the state for what God intended the state to be and do.

These standards also mean that the state cannot encourage irreligion and immorality under the guise of pluralism and separation of church and state. A nation that attempts to make a complete break between the government and morality will end up in anarchy or dictatorship. In either case it will be judged by God. 'Righteousness exalteth a nation: but sin is a reproach to any people' (Proverbs 14.34).

37

GOD WILL SUPPLY OUR NEEDS

'But my God shall supply all your need according to His riches in glory by Christ Jesus' (Philippians 4.19). This promise is as broad as human need; it covers every situation that any believer may face. It is as abounding as the heart of God in the riches of Christ's grace.

We make a number of mistakes in interpreting and applying this promise. We think that God has promised to give us whatever we think we need. We fail to understand actual need because we feel that we know our needs better than God knows them. We often misinterpret material, physical, and temporal needs above spiritual and eternal needs. We become more distraught over loss of goods than over leanness of soul. Hear the words of our Lord, 'Is not the life more than meat, and the body more than raiment?' (Matthew 6.25b).

We sometimes fail to understand this promise in terms of the courses of our lives as they are directed by God. We should know that the promise of Romans 8.28 is another form of the promise that we are considering. 'We know that for the ones who love God – those who are the called ones according to His purpose – God is working all things to a good end.' The course of life may at times be worrisome and distasteful, but God is moving us to His eternal aim for us: 'to be conformed to the image of His Son, that He might be the Firstborn among many children' (Romans 8.29). The end of the journey is the interpretation of the entire journey. The end of the journey is that we be conformed to the image of God's Son.

This promise is as rich as the treasures of heaven, and all the treasures in heaven are in Christ Jesus. 'What, therefore shall we say to these things? If God be for us, who can be against us? He who did not spare His own Son, but gave Him for us all, how shall He not with Him give us by grace all things?' (Romans 8.31, 32). Those who have Christ have all things that God can give. They should not live beneath their privileges (Luke 15.31).

38

NOTHING IN MY HAND I BRING

'For by grace are ye saved through faith; and that not of yourselves: it is the gift of God; not of works, lest any man should boast' (Ephesians 2.8, 9).

The great hymns and gospel songs of the church let us sing our theology. The hymns of John and Charles Wesley have probably influenced the theology of the church as much as their preaching and teaching. An especially significant contribution from another song writer is 'Rock of Ages' by August M. Toplady. In the second stanza the author reviews the devices of human payment of debt and rejects them all as inadequate and even sinful.

> Not the labors of my hands,
> Can fulfill thy law's demands;
> Could my zeal no respite know,
> Could my tears forever flow,
> All for sin could not atone;
> Thou must save, and thou alone.

To offer any of these in an attempt to satisfy the judgment of God or to relieve our consciences is not only foolish; it is also self-righteous.

This song puts the whole question of sin and forgiveness in right perspective. 'Faith is clinging to Christ crucified, laying hold of him with empty hand and renouncing all our own endeavours.'

'Faith is coming to Christ in the nakedness of our guilt and shame, to be clothed in the garment of his righteousness.'

'Faith is looking to Christ in our utter helplessness and casting ourselves on his grace.'

'Faith is fleeing to Christ, foul and filthy as we are, to be washed in the fountain opened for sin and uncleanness.'[3]

---

[3] Frank Colquhoxun, *Hymns We Live By* (Downers Grove, IL: InterVarsity, 1980), p. 102

39

SO, YOU ARE A FREE MORAL AGENT?

Who said you are a free moral agent? Is that what you say, or is that what God says? The fact is that God nowhere says that we are free moral agents.

What the Bible says is that we are servants. Either we are servants of God, or we are servants of the devil. 'Do you not know full well that to whom you give yourselves as servants (for obedience) you are servants to the one whom you obey?' (Romans 6.16). The question answers itself; of course you are the servant of the one whom you obey. There are only two choices: servant of God or servant of Satan.

Being a servant means four things. First, it means that you are not your own. You have given yourself to someone else. In moral and spiritual issues you either belong to God or to the devil. There is no in between.

Second, it means that you have given yourself to obey your master. Your will has been surrendered. So it is no longer a question of free will, but the will of your master – either God or Satan. Third, it means that you are in the position of a bound slave, bound (bonded; hence bond slave) by your master's ownership – either God or Satan. Fourth, it means that you are already committed to a specific goal of life. If you are committed to God in Christ, you are committed to the promises that He has made for eternal life and blessedness. If you have committed yourself to Satan, you are committed to what he has in mind – an eternity of rebellion and judgment.

The word of God is very clear about these two goals. 'The wages of sin is death' (Romans 6.23a). Persons committed to Satan have volunteered themselves to be damned. 'But the gift of God is eternal life through Jesus our Lord' (Romans 6.23b). Persons who have given themselves to Christ have given themselves to everlasting life.

Certainly, there is truth in the claim that we have choices as morally responsible people. However, the fact is that our first choice determines our second choice. The careless boater who lets his craft drift without anchor will drift in the direction of the current. If that current takes the boat toward a waterfall and it gets caught in the rush of water, the boater is no longer in charge. He and his craft will be tossed over the falls. The same thing happens in spiritual choices.

40

WHAT KIND OF PREACHER ARE YOU?

I can hear your protest now, 'I am not any kind of preacher!' But you are, even if you don't like the idea or the word 'preacher'.

John the Baptist was a 'street corner' preacher, or perhaps we should say a 'river bank' preacher. The Apostle Paul was a synagogue and missionary preacher. The Apostle Peter preached to the multitude on the day of Pentecost, and in the household of Cornelius. You and I are preachers.

> You are our letter of recommendation, written on your hearts, to be known and read by all men; and you show that you are a letter from Christ delivered by us, written not with ink but with the Spirit of the living God, not on tablets of stone, but on the tablets of human hearts (2 Corinthians 3.2, 3, RSV).

Aquila and Priscilla were 'tent maker' preachers. They were tent makers by trade, but they are more known for their ministry in the word of God. Paul joined them in tent making and they joined him in ministry. These two first met Paul in Corinth; they followed him to Ephesus, and he left them there. It was in Ephesus that Aquila and Priscilla met Apollos 'an eloquent man, well versed in the Scriptures' (Acts 18.24). These two associates of Paul took Apollos 'and expounded the way of God more accurately' (Acts 18.28). Apollos became an extension of their ministry. Wherever Apollos preached thereafter,

Aquilla and Priscilla also ministered because they had contributed to his spiritual instruction.

This godly couple ministered to Paul in ways that are not recorded in Scripture. Paul says that they risked their own lives in order to save his. Though they were Jews the churches of the gentiles gave thanks for their ministry. They went to Rome (or rather returned to Rome) before Paul was able to get to that city, and there was a church in their house before Paul had ever preached there (Romans 16.3, 4).

It is not God's plan that the gospel spread through the formal exercise of preaching alone. It must be spread from one person to another, from one home to another, from one neighbor to another, from one tradesman to another, from one business to another. This is one of the ways the early church spread; wherever the disciples were scattered even under persecution, 'they went everywhere preaching the word' (Acts 8.4). The Pentecostal movement spread in the same way in the early days of the twentieth century. After all, that is the way Jesus said to do it. 'But ye shall receive power, after that the Holy Spirit has come upon you: and ye shall be witnesses unto me both in Jerusalem and in all Judaea, and in Samaria, and unto the end of this age' (Acts 1.8).

41

WHAT IS REVIVAL?

Revival is a word that is used frequently in the church; in fact, it is used indiscriminately, and has perhaps lost its meaning. It is a restoration of spiritual vigor and holiness of living. The pattern of revival and the signs of revival are the same in all ages of the church – Old Testament and New Testament.

One of the essential aspects of revival is the recognition of the signs that we need to be revived. There are four special signs of the need for revival.
1. Spiritual apostasy by the neglect of worship, powerlessness in prayer and the neglect of thanksgiving and praise.
2. Lethargy – dullness and lifelessness – in which the people of God are unresponsive to the message of the divine Word.
3. Offense at the rebuke of the word of God.
4. Bewilderment at the chastening of the Lord.

These themes of need appear time and time again in the Scriptures.

Notice how the people argue with God about their sins in the books of the prophets, especially in Malachi. 'Wherein hast thou loved us?' (Malachi 1.2). 'Wherein have we despised thy name?' (1.6). 'Wherein have we polluted thee'? (1.7). 'Wherein have we wearied him [i.e. God]?' (2.17a). 'Where is the God of judgment?' (2.17b): 'wherein shall we return?' (3.7). 'Wherein have we robbed thee [i.e. God]?' (3.8). 'What have we spoken so much against thee [i.e. God]?' (3.13). We must examine ourselves to see if these signs of need appear in ourselves and in our congregations.

It was against these signs that the prophets of God spoke and led the people of God in spiritual renewal. The following is a list of the characteristics of biblical revival.

1. An identification and confession of the sins that have drained the spiritual vigor of the people called by God's Name.
2. A broken and contrite heart upon the conviction of sin.
3. A renunciation of sins and confession of God's mercy.
4. A redirection of one's life to a new obedience.
5. A restoration of the place of the word of God in our lives.
6. A restoration of worship, especially in the congregation of the Lord.
7. A renewal of covenant vows to the Lord.

42

ENEMY IN THE HOME

An early episode of the 'All in the Family' show has Archie Bunker in one of his many moralistic diatribes. With a great deal of righteous pomp he points to the Bible which is lying on the television set and he says, 'There is where we get our morals!' Whereupon his wife Edith responds, 'You mean the television set?'

How much truth is there in that statement for your family? We know that we cannot isolate ourselves from reality. We and our children are frequently abused and offended by blasphemy, vulgarity, violence, irreverence, and profanity.

Most of us have a box in the center of our family room that pipes all these things and more into our homes hour after hour. In real life situations when we see these sins, we get a chance to see the whole situation. We can see the disapproval of others, and we often can see the radical consequences of such behavior. In the contrived artificiality of the television program sin is glamorized, vulgarity is accepted and enjoyed as real manliness or womanhood. Profanity (which is our 'polite word for verbal illiteracy') becomes an essential of an expressive vocabulary. People die violently without hurting or bleeding. We don't see the bereaved families. Sexually explicit exposure and activity are touted as normal to dating relationships. Skepticism is accepted as an essential ingredient of sophistication and intelligence. Sometimes all this is mixed with a little pious talk about peace and love, crowned with a heroic deed at the climax.

Where do we get our moral values – the word of God or the television set (or other worldly media)? Perhaps the answer to that question is best given in another question. What is central to our home life, family altar and Bible study or the television set? Please understand that television is not the only culprit here. Look at your magazines, your record (audio cassettes, CDs, etc.) collection, the pictures on your walls, your bumper stickers, the movies you rent or go out to see. We could go on and on, but you get the picture.

43

THIS IS THE LORD'S TABLE

Three things stand out about the Lord's Supper, often called the Eucharist because it is a meal of thanksgiving. The first is the drama of the event. The second is the teaching of this event. The third is its effect.

The drama. The Lord's Supper is the reenactment of the crucifixion of our Lord. It is the drama of redemption. Jesus broke the bread; His body was broken for us. As we break the bread of the Lord's Supper, let us go back to Calvary. See there the Lord is being crucified. His body abused, violated, slain for our sins and healing. Jesus poured the fruit of the vine. Let us go again to Calvary. See there the Fountain of Emmanuel flowing for sin and all uncleanness.

The teaching. The Lord's Supper teaches us about the atonement and promises us that Christ is coming again. We are taught that Christ our Passover has been offered for us. His blood covers and washes away our sins. All the provisions of the atonement are taught here: forgiveness, justification, adoption, the new birth, sanctification, glorification, and healing.

We are taught that Christ will come again. We continue this practice in His physical absence in order to give testimony that He is coming again. By celebrating this supper we celebrate the marriage supper of the Lamb in which we will sit with Christ, with the patriarch, the prophets, and with the redeemed people of all nations, tongues, tribes in the marriage supper of the Lamb.

The effect. In the Lord's Supper we are spiritually nourished. This is a meal. It is designed to do for us spiritually what food does for us physically. As we receive this food and drink let us claim by faith that God's word and Spirit are making us strong and healing us spiritually and physically. God is doing something for our fellowship with one another. To share a meal with another is an act of friendship and love. As we take this meal together, let us share our friendship and love for each other in Christ. We are the family of God eating together.

44

NO WEAPON THAT IS FORMED AGAINST THEE SHALL PROSPER

'No weapon that is formed against thee shall prosper; and every tongue that shall rise against thee in judgment thou shalt condemn. This is the heritage of the servants of the Lord, and their righteousness is of me saith the Lord' (Isaiah 54.17)

'For he shall give his angels charge over thee, to keep thee in all thy ways. They shall bear thee up in their hands, lest thou dash thy foot against a stone' (Psalm 91.11, 12).

God has illustrated these promises throughout Scripture. Righteous Abel was murdered, but God had promised his mother that her seed would bruise the head of the serpent (Genesis 3.15; Romans 16.20). God raised up the line of Seth, which distinguished itself by calling on the name of the Lord (Genesis 4.26).

The line of Seth spread and many of them became corrupt, but out of them God called Abram from Ur of the Chaldees, separating him and his line from pagan surroundings and worship. He gave him and his seed the gospel in covenant (Genesis 12.1-3; Galatians 3.8). God transformed a wandering family, often threatened by nations more powerful than Israel, into a great nation. He protected this family as they walked among their enemies claiming the land for an inheritance from God.

When Egypt threatened Israel with extinction, God nurtured the appointed deliverer in the palace of Pharaoh. When sinfulness threatened to destroy Israel under divine judgment, God supplied an intercessor in this same man Moses.

When greed divided the nation of Israel into two warring nations, God preserved the line of David and the throne of the Messiah. When wicked Queen Athaliah attempted to destroy the seed royal, God raised up Jehoida to protect and preserve the line of David. When seventy years of captivity and dispersion threatened all of Israel, particularly the line of David, God kept alive the line of the Messiah-King. Of this line Jesus was born.

God protected the infant Jesus from Herod by making Egypt His sanctuary. He protected Jesus from many attempts on His life from Bethlehem to Calvary. At Calvary God protected Him in death by receiving His spirit and raising Him from the dead.

All of these events demonstrate God's power and His care. These illustrations are not remote to us; we have inherited the benefits and the deliverances. We are also assured that what God has done in times past is His promise for all times future. What He has done for Israel as the people of God He is prepared and able to do for you and me now. As God guided Israel and lifted her on eagles' wings (Exodus 19.4), He will 'keep thee in all thy ways'. Believe the 'exceeding great and precious promises: that by these ye might be partakers of the divine nature' (2 Peter 1.4) and walk in them.

45

WHERE THERE IS NO VISION THE PEOPLE PERISH

The Apostle Paul is standing before Agrippa. He is on trial for charges that may bring him the death sentence. Normally a defense in such cases would depend on witnesses that would lead to an acquittal, but Paul's defense is 'Whereupon, O King Agrippa, I was not disobedient unto the heavenly vision' (Acts 26.19).

What was this vision that moved this Apostle to such obedience, and to protest a vision as His defense? Was it the vision of souls dying and being damned? No. Was it the vision of his own damnation and fear from his experience on the road to Damascus? No. Was it a vision of himself proclaiming the divine message to eager and hungry audiences? No. Was it the vision of the church spreading to the ends of the earth? No.

All of these visions are needed under certain circumstances. However, they are limited in their appeal and application. They are not significant enough to call for undying zeal and a martyr's death. These visions cannot account for Paul's obedience and defense.

If these visions are not sufficient, what kind of vision is necessary? The only all-sufficient vision is the vision of the crucified, risen, ascended, and returning Lord – the One who appeared to Paul and spoke to him on the road to Damascus. This is the saving vision. Such a vision will lead a man such as Saul of Tarsus to turn from a persecutor to a follower of the way. That vision will be his defense against all charges of heresy and insurrection.

When one has seen this vision, he or she has to tell it even at the risk of life. Paul had to know that retelling this story could lead to his conviction and to death. This vision gives birth to all other visions including the visions listed above. Only in this vision are they legitimate. This is the universal vision: universal in need, application, and significance. It is the empowering vision.

In the centuries since Paul related this experience many more people have seen the same kind of vision. They, like Paul, have given up prosperity, comfort, security (by worldly standards), family, religious connections, homeland, and even life itself.

This vision lies at the heart of our witnessing, our ministry of preaching and teaching, our missionary work, our care for the poor and the infirm. It is the ground of our obedience. Can we say, 'I was not disobedient unto the heavenly vision'? God grant us the grace!

46

HELP! I NEED PRAYER!

'Pray for me, as I pray for you ... We can render one no more effectual service' (William Wilberforce).

Do you have a prayer list? Most of us would probably answer that we do, and we probably keep that list in our minds. This is good, but we are depending on a very faulty system in our greatest service to one another. When someone asks us to pray for them, we agree immediately, breathe a prayer for them at the moment and pray for them only sporadically (if at all) in the coming weeks and months. The needs of our brothers and sisters and of the lost are too important for that kind of inattention. Our service to one another – even our enemies – is too important to be forgotten or to be handled in a slipshod manner.

The advantages of a prayer list are many, but here are a few.

1. It is a reminder to pray.
2. It identifies the person(s) and defines the exact nature of the problem that is to be prayed for.
3. It keeps the person(s) before us so that we are conscious of serving him or her and of loving that person. After all, prayer is an act of love.
4. It is a reminder to do something about those problems that we can relieve by our own actions (to ask forgiveness of those whom we have wronged, to help heal wounds where offense has occurred, to feed and clothe the poor, to speak a

word of encouragement, to write a letter of encouragement).
5. It is a reminder to offer thanks for answered prayer and to praise God for His mighty acts and according to His excellent greatness – to praise God for what He is and for what He does.

The words at the beginning of this meditation were written by a devout man of the eighteenth and nineteenth centuries. He was a powerful force in the British Parliament. He was especially active in the attempt to abolish the slave trade, and is credited as the primary force to abolish slave trading by British merchants. The British Emancipation Act did not pass in Parliament until a month after Wilberforce's death, but He was faithful in prayer and labor. To him this was an essential issue in holiness.

I close this article with a quotation from the words of our Lord. 'Simon, Simon, Satan wanted to take all of you in order to sift you like wheat, but I have prayed for you [individually] that your faith should not fail' (Luke 22.31, 32). Why did Jesus make this specific application? Jesus knew Peter's vulnerability better than Peter did.

As Christ has done for us, let us do for others. Let us pray for one another.

47

THE DEADNESS OF SELF PRESERVATION

Self preservation? It's an oxymoron! Shall we add, 'from a mega moron'?

The life of a seed can be released only if the seed dies. The seed may be kept almost indefinitely if it is protected from moisture and soil. While the seed is being preserved, its life is locked in and is not giving life. Eventually it will lose its life.

Seed that is planted dies. The pith of the seed seems to disintegrate; the skin shrivels and the husk falls away.

The seed that is preserved remains outwardly full and attractive. The owner does not lose it. The seed that is planted disappears. From outward appearances it is lost. It dies, but out of the dying the germ of life produces a plant, and the plant produces fruit and seed – many more than the one seed that died.

This is the order of life seen in Calvary. Jesus had lived a perfect life; He had even been transfigured into the glory of His reward for having lived the perfect life before the Father. He refused to remain on the Mountain of Transfiguration because He had not shared His life through death. So He went from the Mountain of Transfiguration to the Mountain of Death – Calvary. Out of His dying he was raised to the glory of immortality. Out of His death and resurrection He became the Seed of everlasting life for millions who had no life in themselves.

He is life; therefore He gives life. He is love; therefore He gives love. For Him not to give what He is would have been for Him to cease to be the Savior.

God applies this as a moral standard to our conduct. Faith that is not shared is lost. Faith that is shared grows. Material wealth that is not shared is squandered. Material wealth that is shared produces the fruit of love. Love that is not shared is selfishness. Love that is shared abounds. Wisdom that is not shared is reduced to silly riddles. Wisdom that is shared becomes deeper. Strength that is not shared becomes weakness. Strength that is shared becomes stronger. Life that is not shared falls apart. Life that is shared produces life, even if it must do so through dying.

Individuals, congregations, and denominations often face financial crises. It is easy for them to rationalize that they cannot afford to give to evangelism, world missions, poverty stricken areas and people, disaster victims, etc. We cannot afford the 'luxury' of keeping our faith to ourselves and our material goods for ourselves. If we ever let our vision narrow to our own needs many souls will perish. We will perish with them.

48

PRAYER

'I exhort therefore, that, first of all, supplications, prayers, intercessions and giving of thanks be made for all men' (1 Timothy 2.1).

The following lists will be helpful reminders for us of the need for and the purposes of prayer.

Prayer Is Encounter with God, Conversation with God, and Exposure of Ourselves to God.

1. Prayer is wrestling with God (Genesis 32.24; Hosea 12.4).
2. Prayer is by and in the Spirit of grace and supplications (Zechariah 12.10).
3. Prayer is the relationship of a child to his or her father (Matthew 6.5-13).
4. Specific answers are promised to prayer (Matthew 7.7; 21.22; Mark 11.24; James 5.16).
5. The Holy Spirit is promised when we ask in prayer (Luke 11.9-13).
6. The Holy Spirit makes intercession for us (Romans 8.26-27).
7. We are to pray in the Holy Spirit (1 Corinthians 14.15; Ephesians 6.18; Jude 20).
8. Prayer is to be joined with thanksgiving (Philippians 4.6; Colossians 4.2; 1 Thessalonians 5.17).
9. Faith is cultivated by prayer (Jude 20).
10. God answers prayer in relation to specific needs.
    a. God heard the groaning of the children of Israel in Egypt and sent Moses for their deliverance (Exodus 6.5; Acts 7.34).

    b. God promised that if the oppressed cried to Him, He would hear because His is gracious (Exodus 22.23-27).
    c. God showed His glory to Moses when he prayed (Exodus 33.17-23).
    d. God promised Israel that He would hear from heaven, forgive their sins, and heal their land when they prayed (2 Chronicles 7.14).
    e. God will give the desires of our heart and direct our paths (Proverbs 37.4, 5).
    f. He will deliver from trouble (Psalm 86.5; 102.17-20).
    g. He will give wisdom to those who ask (Proverbs 2.3-5), wisdom especially in relation to temptation (James 1.5-7).
    h. He will supply all our need according to His riches in glory by Christ Jesus (Philippians 5.19), even providing whatsoever we desire (Mark 11.24; John 15.17).
    i. He will do exceedingly, abundantly above all that we ask or think (Ephesians 3.20).
    j. He will give mercy and grace to help in time of need (Hebrews 4.16).
    k. He will draw near those who draw near Him (James 4.8).
    l. He will forgive sins and heal the sick; the effectual fervent prayer of the righteous avails much (James 5.16).

God Has Answered Prayer in all the Circumstances of Human Need.
  1. Israel cried unto the Lord and trusted in Him; He delivered them (Psalm 22.4, 5).
  2. The psalmist cried to the Lord, and He healed him and delivered his soul (Psalm 30.2).

3. The psalmist cried to God and God delivered him from his fears (Psalm 34.4).
4. Jonah prayed from the belly of the great fish and the Lord delivered him (Jonah 2.5-7).
5. Jesus heard the prayer of the dying thief, and promised to meet him in paradise (Luke 23.42, 43).
6. Paul asked that his 'thorn in the flesh' be removed and God gave him grace to bear it (2 Corinthians 12.8).
7. Elijah prayed and it rained not; He prayed and it rained (James 5.17; 1 Kings 17).
8. Abraham prayed for the deliverance of Lot and for the saving of the cities; God saved Lot and brought judgment on the cities (Genesis 18).
9. Moses prayed for victory over the Amalekites and God gave Israel victory as Moses prayed (Exodus 17.8-14).
10. Moses stood between Israel and the wrath of God, and God spared the nation (Numbers 11.1-3).

These Are the Exceeding Great and Precious Promises of God by which We Have Been Made Partakers of the Divine Nature (2 Peter 1.4).

1. Faith comes by hearing and hearing by the word of God (Romans 10.17).
2. The Word is near you, even in your mouth and in your heart (Romans 10.8).
3. The Word will accomplish that purpose for which God sent it (Isaiah 55.11).

Note. These are random notes (and in some cases repetitious), but they will provide a guide for your devotional study of prayer and your engagement in prayer.

49

ARE PRAYERS JUST PIOUS NONSENSE? (SOMETIMES THEY ARE.)

We repeat forms without knowing or thinking of their meaning. We can be half-way through some of these prayers without realizing it. We can't recall what we have said. We can hardly realize that we have started to pray.

We repeat vows to which we are not committed. We offer to say what God wants us to say, but we do not sanctify the tongue. We offer to obey God in all things and we have never come to the agony of absolute surrender to His will. We offer to witness and we do not seek the anointing, and we do not seek people to whom we can witness.

We hide our guilt in meaningless and generalized confession. It is easy to say that we have sinned when there is no particular sin in mind. It is quite different to confess, 'My words on that occasion were sinful'; 'My action was unholy', or 'My heart is corrupt and hateful'. Confession that does not bring us before the judgment seat of Christ is a farce.

We hide our bitterness in pious mouthings of happiness and blessedness – happiness and blessing that we do not actually experience. Whom are we fooling: ourselves, our brothers and sisters, our family, our God. If we are fooling anyone, it is ourselves. Look at the honesty of prayers in the book of Psalms. In these prayers and hymns there are agonizing confessions of bitterness. Bitterness is never right, and it is not justified in the Scriptures; but hidden bitterness is not purged from the soul.

We ought not be afraid to come to our heavenly Father in the simplicity of a child who tells everything to his or her parents. God is our Father, and a tender, loving, and understanding Father He is. He is

> merciful and gracious, slow to anger and plenteous in mercy. He will not always chide: neither will he keep his anger forever ... Like as a father pitieth his children, so the Lord pitieth them that fear him. For he knoweth our frame; he remembereth that we are dust (Psalm 103. 8, 9, 13, 14).

With a Father such as this we do not need to play act.

50

LET CHRIST BE LIFTED UP

'And I, if I be lifted up will draw all men unto me' (John 12.32).

From Bethlehem you can see the Cross. The manger is the low point at which the Son of God entered the world. Few would have seen it; probably no one would have recorded it except for Calvary and the resurrection.

From Calvary you can see heaven and eternity. Of this moment Jesus had said, 'For this cause came I unto this hour' (John 12.27). To the dying thief He promised eternity and paradise. 'Today shalt thou be with me in paradise' (Luke 23.43). Of Himself He cried, 'Father, into thy hand I commend my spirit' (Luke 23.46).

From the Cross, you can see the world as the world can see Calvary. 'Jesus of Nazareth the King of the Jews' was written on the Cross in Hebrew, Greek, and Latin (John 19.19, 20). In His prayer 'Father, forgive them; for they know not what they do' (Luke 23.24), Jesus reaches from the throne of God and the altar of God to the dying thief, to the Roman centurion, to the repentant Peter – to all ages, races, social levels, and to every degree of sin.

From Calvary you can see Bethlehem. The life of Christ unfolds before the Cross. His birth, His teaching and preaching, His miracles, His attacks on sin, His forgiving of sins, His rebuke of His disciples, His comfort of His disciples, His baptism, His Transfiguration, His triumphal entry into Jerusalem and Gethsemane.

From Calvary you can see the empty tomb and the Mount of Olives from which Jesus would ascend to the Father. From Calvary you can hear the promise of angels, 'This same Jesus, which is taken up from you into heaven, shall so come in like manner as ye have seen him go into heaven' (Acts 1.11). The King is coming and you can see Him from Calvary.

As Bethlehem is the low point at which Christ enters the world, Calvary is the high point from which He leaves the world to come again.

'And unto them that look for him shall he appear the second time without sin unto salvation' (Hebrews 9.28b).

51

SAFETY AND SECURITY

What are security and safety? In ages past society has answered variously – a large tribe, many archers, many horsemen and chariots, and walled cities. Today we answer in much the same way – large armies, a strong nuclear striking force, a powerful navy, a sophisticated air force, adequate warning system, and an unlimited supply of oil. These are conceptions for national security and safety.

Attitudes about personal security and safety differ very little from the lists above. People suppose that personal and family security and safety are provided by personal strength, physical health, financial assets, job security, good locks, and a fail-safe alarm system and many other temporal devices.

In all ages God has been offended by human attempts to create security. This is true in terms of temporal and physical matters, and it is true of spiritual matters. Our attempts to be our own security push God out of our lives even if we continue to give Him lip service. We substitute human strength for divine strength, and our promises to ourselves instead of God's promises.

We cannot be vigilant enough to insure our own safety. 'Except the Lord build the house, they labour in vain that build it: except the Lord keep the city, the watchman waketh but in vain. It is vain for you to rise up early, to sit up late, to eat the bread of sorrows: for so he giveth his beloved rest' (Psalm 127.1, 2). God promises, 'Behold the eye of the Lord is upon them that fear him, upon them that hope in his mercy' (Psalm 33.18). The eye of the Lord is upon everything that surrounds or approaches those who trust in Him. God's watchfulness gives us complete protection: physical or spiritual and temporal or eternal.

> Behold, he that keepeth Israel shall neither slumber nor sleep. The Lord is thy keeper; the Lord is thy shade upon thy right hand. The sun shall not smite thee by day, nor the moon by night. The Lord shall preserve thee from all evil; he shall preserve thy soul. The Lord shall preserve thy going out and thy coming in from this time forth, and even for evermore (Psalm 121.4-8).

Our Lord emphasized that we should live our lives in this kind of expectancy. Our heavenly Father feeds the birds. He gives the lily its beauty. 'Therefore take no thought saying, What shall we eat? Or What shall we drink? or, wherewithal shall we be clothed? (For after all these things do the Gentiles seek) for your heavenly Father knoweth that ye have need of all these things' (Matthew 6.31, 32).

52

ATONEMENT

How does God forgive?
- By suffering the consequences of human sin;
- By the act of giving His Son to the sinful will of humankind to crucify Him;
- By entering into the cause-effect stream of human sin and by His love triumphing over both the cause and the effect of sin;
- By not only substituting His Son for our sins, but also substituting
- His own agony for our agony in sin.

In all of this the agony is that which is brought on by our sins. Neither Christ nor His Father deserved this pain.

The agony in the heart of God which our sins caused is, in part, the atonement for our sins.

The agony which our sins cause is reflected in:
- the shedding of Christ's blood;
- the heartbreak of the Son in His cry, 'My God, why hast thou forsaken me?'
- the heartbreak of the Father in hearing this cry of His Son.

How do we forgive sins committed against us?
- by recapitulating the way of the Cross;
- by doing what the Father and the Son did in their provision of our forgiveness
- by giving up the greatest treasure of our heart to the consequences of being sinned against;

- by giving ourselves to the pain which the offender inflicts;
- by embracing both the pain and the offender who inflicts the pain;
- by embracing the pain of the offense and in that pain forgiving and embracing.

The Cross for God and for us is a judgment, but it is also an embracing:

'Father, forgive them.'

This is loving as God loves and forgiving as God forgives.

This is a hard saying, but we learn obedience through suffering as Christ did.

53

THE GOSPEL IN MINIATURE: JOHN 3.16

All the elements of the good news are here. Yet it is so amazing that we can hardly believe it. 'It's too good to be true.' But it is true.

God wants us to know that He loves us. That Creator loves creature is unique to the Judeo-Christian religion. In other systems the 'gods' do not love the creature; more often they despise the creature, especially the human creature.

God knows all of creation; He created all things out of His love, and He loves everything that He made. If He knows the flight and fall of the sparrow (and He does, Matthew 10.29-31); if He feeds them (and He does, Matthew 6.26); if God gives the beauty to the lilies and clothes the grass of the field (and He does, Matthew 6.29-30), how much more does He care for those made in His image? Birds, lilies, and grass are not capable of returning love to God, but we are. He is drawn to us because we are made like Him.

Some fear that God will stop loving them if they sin, but this is a lie. Look at what He did in the Garden of Eden; He promised to crush the head of the serpent and save the seed of the woman (Genesis 3.15). Would you stop loving your child for his/her disobedience? Certainly not! God is greater than we.

God tells us that He did not stop loving us and does not stop loving us when we sin. 'For God so loved the world that He gave His only begotten Son that whosoever believeth in Him should not perish, but have everlasting life' (John 3.16). 'But God commendeth His love toward us, in that, while we were yet sinners, Christ died for us' (Romans 5.8; note also Romans 5.6). 'I write these things to you, my little children, that you sin not, but if anyone sins, we have an advocate with the Father, Jesus Christ the righteous One' (1 John 2.1).

We cannot sin without consequences because God's holiness and love are not indulgent. God will not encourage presumption on His grace, but He loves us too much not to chasten us (Hebrews 12.6).

Sin does change the relationship of love, but God does not stop loving us. He loves us as a grieved and grieving Father. Look at the story of the prodigal son – how his father received him when he returned. The father still remembered how his son walked, because a loving father does not forget the peculiar walk of a loved child. When he saw his returning son from a great way off, he knew him (Luke 15.11-32).

God wants us to know how much He loves us. He loves us so much that He keeps on loving us even when we sin. He follows our disobedient ways with a broken heart and weeping eyes. Does God suffer? Yes, when His Son dies. Does God suffer? Yes, when we trample that blood under foot (Hebrews 10.29).

He loves us so much that He made the way for us to come back to Him.

54

CHRIST'S RETURN

The scoffer uses the long absence of Jesus as a basis for doubt and denial. For those of us who know the Lord and His faithfulness, His absence is His promise to return because He said, 'If I go and prepare a place for you, I will come again and receive you to myself; that where I am there ye may be also' (John 14.3). The longer we wait the greater the sense of the imminence of His coming again.

We also know the Lord's 'time table'; one day with the Lord is as a thousand years and a thousand years as one day (2 Peter 3.9, 10). We know that one reason for His delay is His mercy – that none should perish but that all should come to repentance. In these terms the wait has not been long at all.

Until the day of His return, we have the witness of His ministry in the heavenly holy of holies. On the day of atonement in ancient Israel, the congregation watched as the high priest entered the holy of holies. They could not see him and they knew that he carried the burden of the sins of Israel (including His own sins) into the presence of God; this could mean death or it could mean forgiveness – atonement. The only way they could know that their priest was still alive was to hear the sound of the bells on his garments as he ministered before the Lord.

Our high Priest has gone beyond the veil; we no longer see Him, but we do hear the sound of His ministry on our behalf; that sound is the coming of the Holy Spirit upon His people. As long as we hear that sound we know that Jesus is alive. 'Therefore being by the right hand of God exalted, and having received of Father the promise of the Holy Ghost, he hath shed forth this, which ye now see and hear' (Acts 2.33). By the moving of the Holy Spirit we have the witness that He is alive and the assurance that atonement is being provided for us; as long as we hear that sound, we are confident of our salvation and of His coming again. The promise of Scripture is, 'And to them that look for him shall he appear the second time without sin unto salvation' (Hebrews 9.27).

55

THE JOURNEY OF THE MAGI

The wise men crossed many miles and in sincerity stopped to inquire at Jerusalem about the birth of the King whose star had guided them from their far eastern country. They did not find the King whom they sought; so Jerusalem was not the end of their journey. Their journey would not end until they had seen Jesus.

So we must know that our journey is not complete until we have seen Jesus. Until that time, Calvary is our only home. When we do see Him, we will be home. At that point He shall change our vile bodies that they may be fashioned like unto His glorious body (Philippians 3.21). Though we can have no full understanding of what we shall be, we do now that when He appears we shall be made like Him for we shall see Him as He is (1 John 3.1-3).

The way that we live until that time is determined by the goal of holiness. So everyone that has this hope in Him purifies himself or herself even as He is pure. The journey must participate in the goal; if holiness is the goal, holiness is the way.

56

ENCOUNTER WITH GREATNESS

In her book, *Carver: a Life in Poems*, Marilyn Nelson has a poem entitled 'A Patriarch's Blessing' (1905).[4] It describes a reunion between George Washington Carver and his former owner and adoptive father Moses Carver. This poem prompted the thoughts below.
   There are some great people I wish I had known.
Moses and Susan Carver,
George Washington Carver,
Susanna Wesley,
A slave girl who prayed for her white master when he beat her,[5]
C.S. Lewis,
T.S. Eliot,
And many more.
There are some great people whom I have known,
But I had no idea that they were great.
I am sorry!

---

[4] Marilyn Nelson, *Carver: A Life in Poems* (Asheville, NC: Front St., 2001), pp. 54, 55.
[5] 'A Slave Woman's Prayer,' (1816), in J.M. Washington, *Conversations with God* (New York: Harper Collins Publisher, 1994), p. 19. The prayer:

> O Lord, bless my master. When he calls upon thee to damn his soul, do not hear him, do not hear him, but hear me – save him – make him know he is wicked, and he will pray to thee.

> I am afraid, O Lord, I have wished him bad wishes in my heart – keep me from wishing him bad – though he whips me and beats me sore, tell me of my sins, and make me pray more to thee – make me more glad for what thou hast done for me, a poor [N]egro.

57

CHRIST IN YOU THE HOPE OF GLORY

It is better to strengthen
Than to be strengthened.

It is better to comfort
Than to be comforted.

It is better to heal
Than to be healed.

It is better to give patience
Than to receive patience.

It is more blessed to forgive others
Than to be forgiven by them.

It is more blessed to love
Than to be loved.

Share the strength that you have
And you will become stronger.

Give comfort and you will be comforted.

Heal and you will be healed.

Be patient and you will grow in patience.

Forgive and you will be forgiven.

The strength which you receive is from God.

The comfort which you receive is from the Holy Spirit.

The healing which you receive is from the
Balm of Gilead.

The forgiveness which you receive is from the
Blood of Christ who prayed,
'Father, forgive them.'

The love that you receive is from God who is love.

58

JOURNEY TO THE KINGDOM

'There are some standing here that will not taste of death until they see the kingdom of God' (Luke 9.27).

During holy week we like to trace the steps of Jesus from the time He entered Jerusalem until He was crucified. This is a fruitful devotional study: from the Triumphal Entry to the Crucifixion.

I want to focus on a greater journey: the journey from Galilee to the kingdom of God. I take my cue from the point of the following statement: 'There are some standing here that will not taste of death until they see the kingdom of God' (Luke 9.27).

Jesus has just called out the disciples in the Great Confession that He is the Christ of God (Luke 9.20). He followed this with the prediction of His coming, suffering, death, and resurrection (Luke 9.22). Then He invited His disciples to take up the Cross daily and to follow Him.

After He had made some very pointed exhortations and warnings about their discipleship, He made the promise of their seeing the kingdom. So, the so-called 'Travel Narrative' in Luke begins with this promise (not at Luke 9.51 as most commentaries say).

Luke clearly intends us to see the story of the Transfiguration in this way. Because he says, 'About eight days after these sayings; he took Peter, John and James, and went up into a mountain to pray' (Luke 9.28).

Prayer is already experiencing the end of the journey. It is the end of the journey standing on our doorstep!

Notice the relation of prayer in the following events: Jesus prayed after His water baptism, after the temptations in the wilderness, while He was returning from Galilee in the power of the Holy Spirit, the entire night before He called the Apostles, before He made the promise of the Holy Spirit to those who pray, seek, and ask (And there are other instances).

So, it is not surprising that Luke tells us that Jesus was transfigured during a time of prayer). He was translated from time to eternity. Later, Peter would describe this event in these words: 'For we have not followed cunningly devised fables when we made known to you the power and coming of our Lord Jesus Christ, but were eyewitnesses of His majesty. For he received of God the Father honor and glory, when there came a voice to him from the excellent glory, This is my beloved Son in whom I am well pleased' (2 Peter 1.16-17).

Prayer is the paradigm for entering the kingdom of God. We receive the first fruits of the kingdom, the earnest of the Holy Spirit, by asking the Father to give us the Holy Spirit: 'If ye then, being evil, know how to give good gifts unto your children: how much more shall your heavenly Father give the Holy Spirit to them that ask Him' (Luke 11.9-10). Jesus had already said, 'Ask ... seek ... knock' (Luke 11.9-10). Askers receive; seekers find; knockers have the door opened to them.

The exclamation point at the end of the story is Luke 9.51, 'And it came to pass, when the time was come for him to be received up, He steadfastly set his face to go to be crucified,' but that is the way to the fulfillment of the kingdom.

The Hebrews commentary on this event is, 'Let us lay aside every weight, and the sin that doth so easily beset us, and let us run with patience the race that is set before us, looking unto Jesus, the Originator (Author) and Perfecter of our faith, who instead of the joy that was set before him endured the Cross, despising the shame, and is set down at the right hand of the throne of God' (Hebrews 12.1-2).

So, Jesus descended the mountain of glory (Transfiguration) in Order to ascend the mountain of humiliation and suffering (Calvary). The journey to Calvary was not just the trek from the city gate of Jerusalem to a hill called Calvary outside the city. It was a journey from this age to the age that is to come.

His journey took Him from glory to suffering; from immortality to death. His journey is our journey. For a little while, He was made lower than the angels for the suffering of death in order to taste death for every one of us. When He reached the nadir of our dying, He ascended to the Zenith of His resurrection and ours.

Now, He is seated at the right hand of God, and He has brought us with Him. Now we sit together with Him in His resurrection and ascension glory, And the Cross is essential to each step of the journey.

59

A BURNING COAL FROM THE ALTAR (ISAIAH 6)

In the midst of my grief for the death of King Uzziah, You reveal your glory.

Your glory is ablaze with glory because Your Presence adorns it.

A garment of holiness enshrouds You, and it fills the temple of Your praise.

Seraphim are awed by the heaviness of Your holiness.

They hide their faces and their feet from such wonder.

They encircle Your throne while they fly all around You.

They raise their voices in thundering doxology.

> Holy, Holy, Holy is the Lord of hosts.
> The whole earth is full of Your glory.
> And they have been doing this since their creation.
> Before the earth ever was.

Their hunger to glorify You cannot be satisfied; so the praise Goes on and on for eternity.

The heaven of the heavens cannot contain You;

> So the whole earth is filled with your glory.

The foundations of the earth and the heavens tremble at the Sound of such praise.

> And so do I.

Why? Because I am a person of unclean lips,
    And so are the lips of all those around me!
Why am I so troubled by what I see?
    My eyes have seen glory beyond measure—
    The King, the Lord of hosts.
Then, a strange comfort overwhelms me.
    A burning coal from the eternal altar touches my lips.
    I am clean; my lips have been purged!
    So has my heart!
The Spirit of judgment and burning has touched my lips.
    I am clean. I am clean? I am clean!
    So is the rest of Zion, but not yet.
Then I heard a voice.
    Whom shall I send?
    Who will go for Us?
Out of the depts. of my soul irresistible words rush to my lips.
Here am I. Send me. Please send me.
    But what shall I say as I go?
Say to them,
    Hear but remain deaf.
    See but remain blind.
This is My judgment on them.
    They choose not to hear Me; they shall remain deaf.
    They choose not to see; they shall remain blind.

> The dullness of their hearing is My judgment.
>
> > They must not be healed yet.
>
> But Lord, this is an impossible task.
>
> > How long shall I do this?
>
> Until my people have been purged of their chaff;
>
> > Until the cities are wasted;
> >
> > Until their houses are empty;
> >
> > Only a tenth remains.
> >
> > It too shall be burned.
>
> Only a stump shall remain. It is my holy Seed.
>
> Then you can rest; there remains a Sabbath of rest for the people of God.
>
> Lord, I cannot rest until that day You give me rest.

60

A Parable of Christmas

A certain man had lived in his community all his life. He had grown up there, married and now has a child – an only child, a boy. This is a child in whom the father sees great potential. He pours all his fatherly affections into the boy. The child responds with equal love. When the boy looks admiringly at his father, the father beams with pride and satisfaction. He feels like his is the most loved father in the world. This man's relationship to his community has been one of love and service. He has fed the hungry, clothed the poor, provided medical attention to the sick, sought healing for the sick and wounded – even for those who did not appreciate, believe in or return his love. He has given all he could, except his son. But this community despises both the father and the son, especially the son. The father has taught his son to forgive all those who despise him, and the son follows his father's heart and behavior.

Finally, the anger and jealousy of the community turns into fierce hatred and become violent. A crowd from the community surrounds the house, and shouts hateful and wounding words. They move against the house, beating at the doors and windows in order to carry out their hatred on the members of the household, especially this only son. They yell and throw stones into the windows. They swear; they curse heaping abuse on abuse on the son and his father.

The father has only two options for stopping this attack. He could destroy the crowd; he is well able to do this with the power that he has. Or he could provide one last gift to his community – this gift will relieve them of their hatred and create love in its place. The crowd does not want this gift because they have loved to hate.

This gift will break the father's heart; it is the giving of his one and only son to be done with as the crowd's hatred demands. He can give his son to be abused and killed in order to save his and his son's enemies. He can even heal their hatred and cleanse them of this corruption.

Would you do that?
Would I do that?
Would God do that? He would and He did.

For God so loved the world that He gave His only begotten son that whosoever believeth in Him should not perish but should have everlasting life.
John 3.16

INDEX OF BIBLICAL REFERENCES

OLD TESTAMENT

Genesis
3.1-7	69
3.15	87, 107
4.26	87
12.1-3	87
18	97
32.24	95

Exodus
6.5	95
17.8-14	97
19.4	88
22.23-27	96
33.17-23	96

Numbers
11.1-3	97

Joshua
1.7	53
1.9	53

1 Kings
17	97

2 Chronicles
7.14	96
20.15b	54

Psalms
8.4	25, 32
22.4	96
22.5	96
30.2	96
33.18	103-104
34.4	97
85.10	19
91.11-12	87
103.8	100
103.9	100
103.13	100
103.14	100
121.4-8	104
127.1	103
127.2	103

Proverbs
2.3-5	96
14.34	72

Isaiah
6	121
40.4	5
42.3	15
54.17	87
55.11	97

Jeremiah
29.7	28

Hosea
12.4	95

Jonah
2.5-7	97

Zechariah
12.10	95

Malachi
1.2	81
1.6	81
1.7	81
2.17a	81
2.17b	81
3.7	81
3.8	81
3.13	81

NEW TESTAMENT

Matthew
1.18	19
1.19	19
5.3-12	9
6.5-13	95
6.12	11
6.25b	73
6.26	107
6.29-30	107
6.31	33, 104
6.32	33, 104
6.33	33
7.7	95
7.12	50
10.29-31	107
11.30	64
16.25	1
20.28	39
21.22	95
26.33	25
28.19	67
28.20	67

Mark
1.12	69-70
1.13	69-70
1.14-15	67
10.45	39
11.24	95, 96
12.17	71

Luke
1.30	19
1.35	19

Luke, continued

1.45	19	7.34	95	14.1	3
4.1-13	70	8.4	80	14.15	95
4.14	70	17.22	56	15.20-28	48
4.18-19	66	18.24	79	15.54-58	48
9.20	117	18.25	79		
9.22	117	19.19	101	**2 Corinthians**	
9.27	117	19.20	101	3.2-3	79
9.28	117	26.19	89	3.3	62
9.51	41, 117, 118			4.5	40
		Romans		5.20	66
11.1-4	41	1.4	47	10.12	25
11.4	11	1.5	53	12.8	97
11.9-10	118	1.14	68		
11.9-13	95	1.15	68	**Galatians**	
14.31	9	4.17	29	3.8	87
15.11-32	108	4.25	45, 47	6.1	11
15.31	74	5.5	3	6.7	64
22.31	92	5.6	108	6.8b	64
22.32	92	5.6-11	45		
23.24	101	5.8	108	**Ephesians**	
23.42	97	6.8-11	47	1.20-23	47
23.43	97, 101	6.16	77	2.1	47
23.46	101	6.23a	78	2.8	75
		6.23b	78	2.9	75
John		8.17	10	3.20	96
1.29	67	8.26-27	95	4.8-12	48
3	15	8.28	73	6.18	95
3.16	19, 45, 107, 108, 126	8.29	73		
		8.31	74	**Philippians**	
		8.32	74	1.29	9
10.18	45	10.8	97	2.5-11	39
12.27	101	10.17	29, 97	2.9	47
12.32	101	13.1	71	2.10	47
14.3	109	13.1-8	72	2.12	69
15.13	45	13.4	71	2.13	69
15.17	96	16.3	80	3.10	9
17	37	16.4	80	3.11	9
		16.20	87	3.21	111
		16.26	53	4.6	95
Acts				4.8	60
1.8	67, 80	**1 Corinthians**		4.19	73
1.11	102	10.13	70	5.19	96
2.1-4	48	13.4	3		
2.32	48	13.5	3	**Colossians**	
2.33	110	13.13	3	4.2	95
2.34	48				

1 Thessalonians		7.25	44	2 Peter	
5.17	95	9.27	110	1.16-17	118
5.23	37	9.28b	102	1.4	88, 97
		10.29	108	3.9	109
1 Timothy		12.1-2	119	3.10	109
1.7	23	12.6	108		
2.1	27, 95	13.15	57	1 John	
2.1-4	72	13.16	60	2.1	108
2.2	27			2.8-11	61
2.5	39	James		3.1-3	111
2.6	39	1.5-7	96	3.2	37
		3.17	24	3.23	61
2 Timothy		3.18	24	4.16	17
3.12	9	5.17	97	4.18	3
		4.8	96		
Hebrews		5.16	95, 96	Jude	
1.3	56			20	95
2.3	39	1 Peter			
2.4	39	1.1-11	38	Revelation	
4.13	57	4.13	9	5.13	13
4.15	58	4.14	9	22.20	38
4.16	58, 96				

www.ingramcontent.com/pod-product-compliance
Lightning Source LLC
Chambersburg PA
CBHW062008070426
42451CB00008BA/273